THE INSTRUCTIONAL PLAYBOOK

The Missing Link for Translating Research into Practice

JIM KNIGHT | ANN HOFFMAN | MICHELLE HARRIS | SHARON THOMAS

DEDICATED TO

The many educators who have taught us so much and who continue to teach us every day— your ideas, your passion, and your commitment to children are at the heart of any playbook. You inspire us to be better.

Copyright © 2020 by Instructional Coaching Group.

Published by One Fine Bird Press, Lawrence, Kansas

Edited by Kirsten McBride and Sharon Thomas

Library of Congress Cataloging-in-Publication Data

The Instructional Playbook: The Missing Link for Translating Research into Practice

Jim Knight, Ann Hoffman, Michelle Harris, Sharon Thomas

ISBN 9780578578200

Printed in the United States of America on acid-free paper

Art Direction by Clinton Carlson

Design by Chase Christensen

TABLE OF CONTENTS

PREFACE

In what ways do you want to improve? When we ask this question in our workshops, everyone has an answer. They might be trying to learn Spanish, to qualify for the Boston Marathon, or make the perfect cup of coffee. They might be renovating their living room, doing the paleo diet, getting an advanced degree, or using their Calm app to meditate for 30 minutes every day. As these answers reflect, almost everybody is trying to improve at something. If in doubt, check out the shelves of self-help books in your local bookstore or available online.

The reason why everyone is trying to get better at something, we believe, is that people are wired to improve. Improvement doesn't always mean doing more, even if this may come to mind first; improvement may involve cutting back, reducing the "busyness" of our lives, and countless other things. This book is designed to help people get better at something really important—getting better at the way they support student learning and well-being in schools.

"Getting better" is, of course, a nuanced concept. When someone tells us that we need to get better, it can feel like a barely veiled criticism. "You think I need to get better? You don't think I'm good enough?" But that's not the issue, or at least it shouldn't be. Striving to get better is inherent to our humanity. When we stop learning, growing, and improving, something inside of us dies. Getting better, in contrast, fills us with life.

Nevertheless, improvement can be difficult. To truly improve, we have to face our current reality, and that includes what we're doing well. Sometimes "getting better" means just doing more of what is already working. That is, a large part of getting better involves taking already existing knowledge and integrating it into what we do. This knowledge may come from books, articles, workshops, or coaches. But too often, such knowledge never really becomes a part of our repertoire. Books and articles, like life in general, may be so packed with information that it is difficult to identify what is most important. Similarly, workshops may be packed with great ideas and strategies, but after we leave, we struggle to remember all the information we heard.

So even if we want to implement new ideas, we don't always know how to prioritize and remember everything we read and learn. Enter coaches. Instructional coaches help teachers learn and implement strategies that teachers want to implement to help their students hit powerful engagement or achievement goals. For example, a teacher might implement formative assessment to help students learn to how to write complete sentences. Coaches support teachers in learning new strategies by describing, modeling, and partnering with them to adapt selected strategies until students hit their goals. To do this, coaches need to have a deep knowledge of the strategies they explain and model, and they need tools they can use to enhance explanations and implementation of those strategies.

Enter the instructional playbook.

The instructional playbook, first, is a tool that helps coaches develop the deep knowledge they need in order to be effective. Many coaches are unclear about what teaching strategies they share with teachers. If coaches have the task of supporting teachers as teachers try to get better, then coaches need to know, and know well, the strategies they share. Second, the playbook is a concise collection of tools that coaches create and then use to support teacher learning. We say that an instructional playbook is the missing link for translating research into practice because creating a playbook compels coaches to develop the deep knowledge and the tools they need to support teachers as they learn, implement, refine, and adapt practices to meet their students' needs.

To create this book, which we affectionately refer to as "The Playbook Book," we had to get better, too. We did this, in large part, by interviewing educators who are creating playbooks— their comments and ideas are woven into every part of this book. We are profoundly grateful to all those who generously took time to share what they were learning about the playbook. In addition, we deepened our knowledge by reading and thinking through the ideas of many authors, especially the works of Amy Edmondson, Michael Fullan, Atul Gawande, Heidi Grant-Halvorson, John Hattie, Chip and Dan Heath, Bill Jensen, and Patricia Lauer. Our book is better because their books are so good.

Additionally, we want to point out that we are not done getting better. To keep improving, we would like your help. As you create and implement your own playbooks, you will learn a lot, and we would love to learn with you. Please let us know what you are learning by writing us at hello@instructionalcoaching.com.

Here's to better learning for all of us, and especially the students we serve and support.

ACKNOWLEDGMENTS

FROM JIM KNIGHT

The only reason I'm able to do this work is because of my life and business partner, Jenny. I love you, love our life, and love all that we create together. There are no words that can convey how grateful I am that you are in my life.

Geoff, Cameron, David, Emily, Ben, Isaiah, and Luke—you are my inspiration. This work is for you, your children, and your children's children. It is such a joy to see you growing up and doing great things to make this world a better place for every person.

Ann Hoffman, Michelle Harris, and Sharon Thomas, my co-authors and partners in consulting and writing, thank you for taking this journey with me. I am grateful for your ideas, your warm and forgiving friendship, your unwavering commitment to doing what is best for kids, and the deep sense of purpose you share with all of us at ICG. I have always known how fortunate I am that you are sharing ICG's ideas, and I'm now doubly grateful since you are creating and presenting ICG's ideas.

Chase Christensen and Clinton Carlson, I'm very grateful for your willingness to break the mold and the wonderful design for this book and all of our publications. Dostoyevsky said, "beauty will save the world," and I am so grateful that our work looks so beautiful thanks to your imagination and diligence. Thank you also to Kirsten McBride for editing this book and all my writing. I've never written a page that Kirsten hasn't been able to improve.

I am also deeply grateful to the other members of our growing ICG team—Brooke Deaton, Claudia Kressig, Emily Malatesta, Kevin Kressig, Erin Krownapple, Geoff Knight, Matt Kelly, Steve Lane, Sasha Strunk, and Ruth Ryschon. We all want ICG to be a force for good, and that is only possible with good people. Each one of you is a great person and you all inspire me to be better.

FROM ANN HOFFMAN

Jim and Jenny: You have dedicated your lives to creating a better world for students and teachers. I am inspired by your work and passionate about sharing it. I thank you for the influence you have had on my life and for the responsibility you entrust to me to influence, teach, and inspire. Your influence is only dwarfed by my gratitude. I thank you for being a part of my life as both friends and colleagues. However, I thank you most for your continued work to change lives for the better. I know both of you have done that for me.

I could not ask for better colleagues and friends than Michelle Harris and Sharon Thomas. You are both so knowledgeable, kind, and generous, always willing to share. I know I can count on you to support me especially when I am clearly out of my comfort zone. You have both made me a better person, both personally and professionally, and I am so very grateful.

Jim, my amazing husband, I am unbelievably grateful for your never-ending love, support, encouragement, and most of all your selflessness. You bring out the best in me. You cheer for me, pick me up when I am down, and spoil me to death! You have made my work possible, and you inspire me each day. I could never thank you enough for your unconditional love and support.

To my sons, Aaron and Adam: I am so very proud of the adults you have become. You now inspire me with your kindness, work ethic, and desire to make the world a better place. You have both chosen truly amazing spouses, and I cannot wait to continue to watch your lives unfold. Thank you for always supporting my work.

To my mother and late father: You allowed me the freedom to explore my passions. You always believed in me, encouraged me, inspired me, and of course, shaped my thinking. Most importantly you served as great models of wonderful human beings. Simply, thank you.

To the district leaders and coaches who were willing to go on the journey of creating an Instructional Playbook with me: Thank you for your collaboration, advice, and feedback. Your contributions to this work have been invaluable.

FROM MICHELLE HARRIS

My ICG consultant team Ann Hoffman and Sharon Thomas: I could not ask for better colleagues. Thank you for constantly pushing my thinking, keeping me in check, listening to me, loving me, and making my work environment as perfect as it could possibly be. I cannot believe my good luck and fortune working with the two of you.

Jim Knight: You are the very reason I am able to do what I do. I am forever grateful for our start in Beaverton and all that has arisen since. You have helped shape my career in a way I never thought possible and your mentorship continues to influence me deeply. There are not enough ways to thank you for investing in and believing in me.

Frisco, Texas, coaches and Mary Webb: Thank you for digging into this work with me time and time and time again. You live and breathe Partnership and I am so grateful for you all.

Lastly, the loves of my life: Dave, Porter, and Finlay Harris. Your support, love, and laughter mean the absolute world to me. Thank you for letting me live my work dream even when it means I'm not home every day. I love the three of you fiercely and completely.

FROM SHARON THOMAS

During my years as a teacher and instructional coach, Sherry Eichinger-Wilson and Laura Hullinger were coaches who modeled partnership and integrity every single day. Jean Clark and Michael Hodnicki showed me what ethical leadership looks like, and their example has guided me in many ways ever since.

At ICG, Jim Knight, Ann Hoffman, and Michelle Harris show me how to solve problems creatively and how to navigate new waters with strength and clarity. Their teamwork, kindness, and hilarity make this work even more meaningful for me. Years ago, when I first worked with Jim, he gave me guidance on instructional problems that were troubling me in my classroom. I had no idea then that he would continue not only to help me to understand more about people and schools, but also that he would bring so many wonderful people into my life.

My husband, Randy Cover, handles every challenge in life with unfailing love, support, kindness, and humor (he's even an ace proofreader). Our sons, Andrew and Joseph, were always so loving and understanding at times when Mom needed to be at school for other people's kids instead of being home more with my own. They are their father's sons, and I could not be luckier or more grateful.

ABOUT THE AUTHORS

Jim Knight, Senior Partner at ICG, has spent more than two decades studying professional learning, effective teaching, and instructional coaching. He is a Founding Senior Partner of the Instructional Coaching Group and a Senior Research Associate at the University of Kansas Center for Research on Learning.

Jim's book *Instructional Coaching: A Partnership Approach to Improving Instruction* (Corwin, 2007) was the first comprehensive book focused on instruction coaching, and similarly Jim's book *Focus on Teaching* was the first book-length publication addressing the topic of video and professional development. Jim's other books include *Unmistakable Impact, High-Impact Instruction, Better Conversations*, and *The Impact Cycle*.

Jim's articles on professional learning, teaching, and instructional coaching have appeared in journals such as *The Journal of Staff Development, Principal Leadership, The School Administrator, Kappan,* and *Educational Leadership*. Frequently asked to lead professional learning, Jim has presented to more than 100,000 educators from six continents. He has a Ph.D. in Education from the University of Kansas and has won several university teaching, innovation, and service awards. Jim also writes the Radical Learners blog.

Ann Hoffman, Senior Consultant at ICG, and a Professional Development Leader for the University of Kansas Center for Research on Learning (KU-CRL) with more than 30 years of experience. As one of the first professional developers for KU-CRL as well as one of the first consultants with ICG, Ann has worked with thousands of teachers, coaches, and administrators in the United States and internationally. Ann is a recipient of the Gordon R. Alley Partnership Award and the Strategic Instruction Model Leadership Award, both from KU-CRL. She is also the 2017 recipient of the Don Deshler Leadership Award from the Instructional Coaching Group. In addition, Ann serves as a founding member of the advisory board for the Belin-Blank Center for Gifted and Talented Education at the University of Iowa. Ann lives in Iowa and California with her family.

Michelle Harris, Senior Consultant at ICG, began teaching in El Cajon, California. She taught middle school English and social studies before serving as an instructional coach, Title I coordinator, student manager, and assistant principal at three middle schools, a K-8 school, and a 6-12 IBO school, all in Beaverton, Oregon. A seasoned staff developer, Michelle has presented and keynoted all over the United States and in Europe and Africa. She lives in Portland, Oregon, with her husband and two sons. When not working, she enjoys reading, traveling, attending her sons' numerous sporting events, entertaining friends and family, and sitting in a chair on a sunny beach.

Sharon Thomas, Senior Consultant at ICG, is a National Board Certified English teacher, instructional coach, student advocate, and writer. Along with her work in ICG workshops, Sharon coordinates the ICG Coaching Certification process. She is also a consultant for the Touchstones Discussion Project and a Certified SIM Professional Developer in the area of writing. She is the founder of the Cecil County [Maryland] Teacher Leadership Network and has presented at conferences across North America on the issues of secondary school literacy and teacher leadership. Her experience with teacher leadership in school reform was published in *Principal Leadership*. Sharon lives in Maryland with her family.

EDUCATORS INTERVIEWED

We are very grateful to the educators listed here who agreed to be interviewed for this book. They are knowledgeable pioneers who helped us learn about playbooks by creating their own without the support of this book. The generous input of these educators will go forth with this book, carrying with it an impact greater than we can measure.

Amber Theinel
Math Coach
Franklin Special School District
Franklin, Tennessee

Brooklyn McClaws
Learning Coach
Corral Cliffs Elementary
Washington County, Utah

Ellen Dorsey
Mathematics instructional Coach
Washington Central Advisory
Union 32, Burlington, Vermont

Harrison McCoy
Instructional Coach
Education Service Center
Region 11, White Settlement, TX

Jana Claxton
Professional Development
Coordinator, Irving ISD
Irving, Texas

Dr. Karen Norris
Director of Curriculum and Instruction
Momentous Institute
Dallas, Texas

Lorraine Duitsman
Instructional Coach
Lewis Central High School
Council Bluffs, Iowa

Maureen Hill
Instructional Coach
Murrayville Elementary
Wilmington, NC

Rachel LeForce
Instructional Coach
Kaiser Elementary School
Oklahoma City Public Schools

Tiffany Porter
Learning Coach
Crimson View Elementary
Washington County, Utah

Angie Evans
Learning Coach
Red Mountain Elementary
Washington County, Utah

Christina Woodward
Instructional Coach
Lewis Central High School
Council Bluffs, Iowa

Emily Sicilia
Sr. Professional Learning Specialist
Michigan Virtual
Lansing, Michigan

Hilary Herrmann
Professional Learning Coordinator
Poudre School District
Larimer, Colorado

Dr. Joel Beyenhof
High School Principal
Lewis Central High School
Council Bluffs, Iowa

Kristina Feldner
Professional Development
Coordinator, Irving ISD
Irving, Texas

Mark Dowley
Educator/Coach
Brighton Grammar
Melbourne, Australia

Michele Kavars
Gifted Strategist
MTSS Department of Education
Council Bluffs, Iowa

Robert Proffit
District Coach Supervisor
Washington County, Utah

April Strong
Instructional Coach
Martin County Schools
Stuart, Florida

Darlene Tanner
Elementary Learning Coach
Diamond Valley Elementary
Washington County, Utah

Erin Luckhardt
Professional Learning
Specialist, Michigan Virtual
Lansing, Michigan

Jackie Zimmerman
Secondary Coach Facilitator
Katy ISD
Houston, Texas

Joi Lunsford
Intervention/PLC
& Teacher Support
Canyon Schools, Texas

Lindsay Manzella
Instructional Coach
American International School
of Budapest, Budapest, Hungary

Mary Webb
District Director of
Elementary Instruction
Frisco ISD, Frisco, Texas

Nicole Sjo
Learning Coach
Water Canyon High School
Washington County, Utah

Shannon Hatch
Learning Coach
Sunrise Ridge Intermediate
Washington County, Utah

CHAPTER 1

THE LIFE-CHANGING MAGIC OF THE INSTRUCTIONAL PLAYBOOK

is about

Creating an organizational tool for coaches so they can clearly explain high-impact teaching strategies

by understanding

by knowing

by understanding

Why

What

How

- efficient
- clear
- depth of understanding
- coaching success

- table of contents
- one-page descriptions
- checklists

- process for development
- process for use
- process for communication

THE LIFE-CHANGING MAGIC OF THE

INSTRUCTIONAL PLAYBOOK

 SNAPSHOT:

This chapter offers a big picture description of instructional playbooks. It covers what an instructional playbook is, why it is important, how it is created, who uses it, and how it is used. You can skip this chapter if you know why you need a playbook and if you prefer to learn without a big picture overview of what you are learning.

> **To truly cherish the things that are important to you, you must first discard those that have outlived their purpose.**
> MARIE KONDO

"The clarity that the playbook brings helps teachers intellectually and emotionally feel competent. It also helps coaches feel competent."
////////////.

HILARY HERRMANN

Professional Learning Coordinator for Poudre School District, Fort Collins, Colorado

At the time of this writing, *Tidying Up With Marie Kondo* is a popular program on Netflix, based on Ms. Kondo's popular book, *The Life-Changing Magic of Tidying Up: The Japanese Art of Decluttering and Organizing* (2014). According to Ms. Kondo, a world-renowned tidying expert, "life truly begins after you have put your house in order" (p. 204). On the program, each week she coaches people who have piles and piles of possessions, and by the end of an episode, she helps them clear away the clutter to find more order and joy in their lives.

Some school leaders are a bit like the people in Marie Kondo's program, but instead of hoarding possessions, they hoard teaching strategies. Their intent is unquestionably good; there are so many issues to deal with in a school district, and more strategies always seem needed to help address them. But too often, the more strategies that are proposed, the less teachers implement them, figuring "this too shall pass." To get beyond this impasse, what districts need is a tool to help them "do a Marie Kondo" on their strategies— that tool is the instructional playbook.

What Is an Instructional Playbook?

An instructional playbook is a concise, precise document that summarizes the essential information about evidence-based teaching strategies that instructional coaches use to support teachers and students. In most cases, the teaching strategies in an instructional playbook are at the heart of a district's professional development.

The term "playbook" may be used to describe a script for a play, to document workflow in business, or even as the name for a tablet computer, but the term is best known, at least in North America, for its use in athletics. In sports, playbooks are compilations of plays that athletes rehearse during practice so that when the coach calls out the name of a play during the pressure of a tough game, the players immediately know what to do. Mary Webb, director of elementary instruction in Frisco, Texas, and a Dallas Cowboys fan, identified many similarities between instructional and athletic playbooks in our interview with her.

> I think an instructional playbook is very similar to the playbooks used in football. We're looking at the kids and we're choosing a strategy, hoping that it's going to have a positive impact, just like a football coach would do when he wants to see how to get that ball down the field.

Jim first got the idea for instructional playbooks during an airplane conversation with an executive from a well-known software corporation about coaching and professional learning. As part of the discussion, Jim asked how the firm ensured that people in the organization learned how to do the many different things they needed to do. The executive responded with a simple answer, "We create playbooks."

"Playbooks," she explained, "are clear and concise explanations of the processes and practices our employees implement." Jim took note, and that day the idea at the heart of this book was born.

The most effective playbooks are lean and clean. If playbooks are complicated, filled with complex writing, diagrams, and dozens of teaching strategies, they are less likely to help instructional coaches get the deep knowledge they need to effectively explain and model strategies for teachers. To ensure that playbooks are clear, concise, focused, and therefore easy to use, we recommend that they include only three parts:

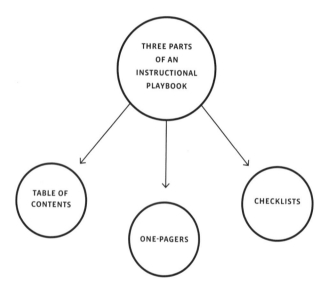

1. A Table of Contents (see CHAPTER 2) that itemizes the teaching strategies included in the playbook.

2. A One-Pager (see CHAPTER 3) for each teaching strategy that explains the purpose of the strategy, the research supporting it, and what the teacher and students are doing during the use of the strategy.

3. A sufficient number of Checklists (see CHAPTER 4) for the teaching strategies in the playbook so that coaches can precisely describe them, thereby making it as easy as possible for teachers to implement them effectively and efficiently.

Why Instructional Playbooks Are Necessary

"Directing attention to where it needs to go is a primary task of leadership."

///////////////.

DANIEL GOLEMAN

Instructional playbooks are organizational tools that coaches use to help them focus on high-impact teaching strategies and then explain those strategies to teachers so the teachers and their students can meet powerful, student-focused goals. Instructional playbooks are typically the missing link in translating research into practice because, even after reading books or attending professional development sessions, too often teachers don't have the specific, practical information they need to implement teaching strategies effectively. To do so, they need the strategies to be translated into explicit, actionable knowledge. Instructional playbooks help make this possible in at least five ways.

1.   **Instructional playbooks help educators identify the highest-impact teaching strategies.** The very act of creating an instructional playbook forces educators to sort through all the strategies they have purchased or disseminated in one way or another and identify those strategies that will have the highest impact on learning and students' well-being. As we explain in CHAPTER 2, identifying the highest-impact strategies involves reviewing the research on practices, identifying typical goals teachers set for students, discussing the specific needs of students, and then choosing no more than 15 to 20 high-yield strategies.

2.   **Instructional playbooks lead to deep knowledge.** Teachers are under constant pressure to implement new teaching strategies, but translating those strategies from books or other sources into action can be difficult and complicated. As a result, teachers often need the support of instructional coaches to acquire the deep knowledge of new strategies. To be effective, instructional coaches and other professional developers need to acquire a deep understanding of the teaching strategies they share, and creating playbooks helps them do just that.

That is, when they create a playbook, coaches need to review the research, identify the core purpose of each strategy, identify how it will be used by teachers and students, and then create checklists that identify important aspects of each strategy. The deep work involved in creating a playbook increases the likelihood that coaches will be more effective and, as a result, that teachers will find it easier to implement new strategies effectively. In short, playbooks help instructional coaches be more successful with teachers, which in turn helps teachers be more successful with students.

3. **Instructional playbooks build a shared vocabulary.** When educators start to create an instructional playbook, they often realize that they do not hold shared definitions of key educational terms. For example, when Ann worked with a group of educational leaders and coaches in a large school district in Texas, it quickly became clear to the people in the room that many of them had very different understandings of the terms "differentiation" and "scaffolding." One of the participants said what no doubt many of the people in the room were thinking, "If we're the leaders in this district and we don't know what these words mean, how can we expect our teachers to implement them?"

Clarifying the meaning of concepts such as differentiation, scaffolding, engagement, growth mindset, etc., helps people see learning and interactions in a clearer way in the classroom. Some words make the invisible, visible. The simple act of talking about and working to develop a shared, deeper understanding is very meaningful professional development.

4. **Instructional playbooks reduce stress.** For some coaches and teachers, the playbook is important because it relieves stress. When some teachers request coaching support, they do so because they feel anxious about something that is or isn't happening in their classroom. So when a coach is able to share some strategies from

a playbook, it can be a stress reliever for the teacher. Additionally, coaches may feel anxious if they don't know what they can do to help teachers. A playbook, in many cases, ensures that coaches are prepared to help teachers with the issue that is most important to them and their students.

5. **Instructional playbooks foster hope.** A final advantage of the playbook is that it is a tool that coaches can use to increase teachers' hope. Shane Lopez, one of the world's leading experts on hope, describes hope as encompassing three factors (2014). First, when people have hope, they have a preferred future, a goal that describes "where [they] want to go, what [they] want to accomplish, who [they] want to be" (p. 24). Second, people who have hope have "agency," a belief that they "can make things happen" (p. 25) and that their actions will enable them to reach their goal. Finally, hope requires pathways, "plans that carry [people] forward" (p. 25).

SHANE LOPEZ'S ELEMENTS OF HOPE

» Goals

» Agency

» Pathways

In many ways, coaches and other professional developers empower teachers to experience hope. Coaches partner with teachers to identify goals and often help teachers to see that they, as Lopez says, "can make things happen." The instructional playbook is important for fostering hope because it documents and clarifies strategies coaches can share with teachers to help them see the pathways to their goals. When a teacher sees that a different approach to questioning may increase his students' cognitive engagement, the teacher begins to have hope.

» Instructional Playbooks help educators identify the highest-impact teaching strategies.

» Instructional Playbooks lead to deep knowledge.

» Instructional Playbooks build a shared vocabulary.

» Instructional Playbooks reduce stress.

» Instructional Playbooks foster hope.

How Instructional Playbooks Are Created

WHO CREATES THE PLAYBOOK?

To get started on a playbook, coaches and their leaders must decide who will contribute to the process:

» Will a team of school- or system-wide coaches work together to create a common playbook for everyone?

» Will grade-level coaches or content-area coaches work with their teams to create playbooks specifically for use in their areas?

» Will school or system administrators, curriculum coordinators, or teachers help decide which teaching strategies will be included?

» Will students or any others in a school be involved in creating the playbook?

Each person brings unique knowledge and expertise to a meeting, so, assuming discussions are effectively organized, the more people who meet to create a playbook, the better the playbook will be—at least up to a point. Also, having more people review the playbook helps ensure that nothing is missed. And, when more people are involved in the collaboration, there will be a deeper understanding across a district of why strategies are included (or not) in the playbook and how strategies increase student achievement and well-being.

"You know, the more brains around it, the better."

//////////////.

JOI LUNSFORD

PLC and Teacher Support Instructional Coach at Canyon Schools in Amarillo, Texas, commenting on the creation of the Canyon Schools instructional playbook

HOW WILL THE PLAYBOOK BE USED?

One of the first questions people ask when they start to think about creating a playbook is, "How will it be used?" Should a playbook be for a single coach, a single school, grade-level coaches (for example, all elementary coaches), content-area coaches (for example, all literacy coaches), or for the entire district?

Our answer is, "It depends."

What matters is that the playbook helps coaches support teachers in hitting their student-focused goals. A playbook filled with strategies that don't help the teachers and students is pretty much a waste of paper (or bytes). If most of the teachers in one school have less than 3 years' experience whereas most of the teachers in another school have more than 15 years' experience, the coaches in those two schools will likely need some different teaching strategies in their playbooks.

At the same time, although a playbook is more useful when it is designed to meet the specific needs of the teachers and students with whom an individual coach works, we suggest that the contents of playbooks be as consistent as possible across a district. When all the coaches in a district know the same strategy, they can share their learning with each other and collaborate more effectively. If all the coaches in a district are experts in the use of learning maps (Knight, 2013), for example, they can grow and learn together and subsequently share what they learn with teachers. On the other hand, when the coaches use different strategies for planning or mapping content, for example, the same kind of collaborative professional learning is not possible.

WHAT IS COVERED IN THE PLAYBOOK?

People often feel compelled to make the playbook more complicated than it needs to be. They may want to add pages and pages of strategies, complex diagrams designed to capture a district's pedagogical framework, or detailed information on why each strategy is important. Unfortunately, when playbooks are too complicated, they often remain on the coach's shelf unused. Similarly, if potential strategies are not thoroughly scrutinized when the playbook is created, the playbook may end up including too many strategies, and as a result, coaches will struggle to develop the deep knowledge they need to help teachers implement the strategies effectively. The most useful instructional playbooks are focused, so creating a great playbook is as much about deciding what not to include as it is about deciding what to include.

Limiting the Table of Contents to one page and the number of components of the playbook to three keeps the focus on the most important strategies and makes it easier for coaches to develop the deep knowledge they need to explain strategies clearly. Keeping the playbook lean, in turn, gives teachers enough information to choose a strategy to hit the goal that they have set for their students without being overwhelmed. A simple playbook is one that coaches can easily use.

HOW IS THE PLAYBOOK CREATED?

CHAPTERS 2, 3, and 4 in this book provide specific information about the process for creating the three components of a playbook, but the process is fundamentally one of editing.

When educators sit down to create the Table of Contents, they start by listing the most common goals that teachers identify during coaching, and they then brainstorm all of the possible strategies that they might share with teachers for those goals. Coaches then shorten that list down to one page of the most relevant and powerful evidence-based teaching strategies for their teachers.

A One-Pager is created for each strategy on the Table of Contents. When educators sit down to write the One-Pager for each strategy, they concisely capture the most crucial information people need

"People get focused through one-page tools...if you can actually get everything on one page...that means the tool and the process caused you to reflect on what it is you want to do...If you limit the number of pages that people have to explain themselves, it forces them to reflect first and think about what they're trying to do. That's very important."

///////////////.

KENT GREENES

from Bill Jensen's Simplicity: The New Competitive Advantage *(pp. 52-53, 2000).*

to know about a teaching strategy. They then edit that document down to one page to ensure that only the most relevant and helpful information is included. Often a One-Pager consists of (a) a single sentence that explains the strategy, (b) a brief summary of existing research on the strategy, (c) a statement of the purpose of the strategy, (d) an explanation of how the strategy is taught, and (e) an explanation of how the strategy is used by students.

Finally, when coaches sit down to create the Checklists section for a strategy, they determine the number of checklists that a particular strategy requires and note all of the possible steps on each of those checklists. They then edit each checklist down to the essential elements while ensuring that they include all steps that are critical for successful implementation. Each checklist should make learning and implementing new strategies easier for teachers; usually checklists serve one of four purposes: (a) they describe how do something, such as how to create learning maps; (b) they describe criteria for excellence, such as the characteristics of effective learning maps; (c) they explain how teachers teach a strategy, such as how to share learning maps with students; and (d) they explain how students are to use or respond to a strategy, such as how students should use learning maps.

The process for creating a playbook is deceptively simple, and each step requires educators to put aside their feelings about favorite (and perhaps less favorite) strategies to create a document that truly meets the needs of the teachers and students coaches serve. And that process is never truly over. As students' needs change (and coaching requests, therefore, change), coaches will need to add and delete strategies to keep pace with those changes. Similarly, as research reveals new information about best practices, coaches will need to ensure that they are providing practices that have strong research support and that they can articulate that support to teachers. Finally, as teachers and coaches partner to implement strategies, over time, better and better practices will emerge.

"Simple can be harder than complex: You have to work hard to get your thinking clean to make it simple. But it's worth it in the end because once you get there, you can move mountains."
//////////////

STEVE JOBS

We view instructional playbooks as living documents that capture organizational learning about teaching strategies. Joi Lunsford, an instructional coach in Amarillo, Texas, talks about her instructional playbook in a similar way: "I don't know if it will ever be complete. It is something that we are constantly editing and updating and tweaking."

Creating a playbook can seem a daunting task, but the playbook will make professional learning clearer, more focused, more explicit, and consequently, more effective. The playbook is an educator's friend, designed to alleviate anxiety, not exacerbate it.

Using an Instructional Playbook

THE PLAYBOOK AND *THE IMPACT CYCLE*

Lisa Pryor supports educators across seven states as part of her work with the University of Oklahoma Outreach, supporting instructional coaching and encouraging a coaching mindset with the educators. But this job is not her first experience with coaching. Lisa's father coached football for many years in Oklahoma, and she remembers his coaching approach well. When she was a child, Lisa would climb into her father's lap, and as she closed in to hug him, she would feel something in his shirt pocket crunch against her face.

That crunch was an index card that he carried with him at all times. On the index card, he had written three words: Face, Solve, Adjust. When a player was struggling in some way and needed refocusing, Coach would hand him the card as a reminder to do three things:

» Face the problem.

» Determine ways to solve the problem.

» Adjust his actions until the problem is no longer a problem.

Lisa's father's approach to coaching college athletes is not a partnership approach in the way that our instructional coaching approach is, but his version of a "coaching cycle" bears a striking resemblance to our Impact Cycle. In our coaching process, instructional coaches partner with teachers to move through three stages that are quite similar to the process advocated by Lisa's father.

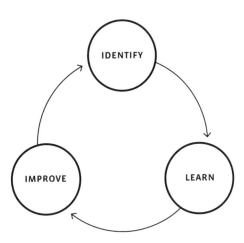

STAGE ONE: IDENTIFY

» identify current reality in the classroom (Face)
» identify a powerful, student-focused goal to address the problem (Solve)
» identify a teaching strategy the teacher will implement to try and hit the goal (Solve)

STAGE TWO: LEARN

» Explain and model the strategy precisely and provisionally, ensuring that teachers are partners in determining how the strategy will be adapted for the unique needs of students (Adjust)

STAGE THREE: IMPROVE

» Make adaptations, which sometimes include changing the teaching strategy or changing how it was taught (Adjust)

Coaches use the instructional playbook in all three stages of the coaching cycle. First, they frequently draw on the playbook to assist teachers in identifying the strategies they will implement to hit their goal. In some cases, teachers know what strategy they want to use, but when teachers are unsure of next steps, coaches can ask, "Would you like me to share some options?" If the teacher says yes, coaches can share some strategies, usually from the playbook, that the teacher can consider using to hit the goal.

Once the teacher has identified the teaching strategy he or she wants to implement to try and hit a goal, the coach can use the checklists from the playbook to explain the strategy. This is helpful in at least two ways. First, if the coach helped create the playbook, he or she will likely have a deep understanding of the strategy, which will make it easier to explain the strategy. Additionally, the checklists from the playbook may be used to precisely explain the strategy, making it easier for the teacher to adapt the strategy and get ready to implement it.

Finally, when teachers implement a given strategy, they usually discover that they need to make adaptations to what they are doing in order to hit the goal. Sometimes the adaptations involve changing how a strategy is taught or choosing a different strategy altogether. Again, the playbook is helpful. Coaches and teachers can return to the original checklist from the playbook to see if the changes they made during implementation decreased the strategy's power. Additionally, they can consider whether other strategies in the playbook might be a better choice for the teacher to use to hit the identified goal.

THE PLAYBOOK AS A COMMUNICATION TOOL

The instructional playbook serves several functions as a communication tool, too. First, it helps leaders in the school better understand what coaches do since the teaching strategies in the playbook are chosen to address the goals most frequently identified by teachers working with coaches. When school and district leaders collaborate with teachers to identify what to include in the Table of Contents they gain deeper insight into the complex, important work done by coaches. That kind of collaboration establishes trust between teachers, coaches, and teachers.

Second, the existence of the playbook makes it easier for new coaches to quickly learn the focus and the teaching strategies considered high impact in a district. For example, a coach who comes to a district that has an instructional playbook will be much better prepared to partner with teachers and provide the instructional coaching support necessary to meet goals.

Finally, when a playbook is created district-wide, it communicates the instructional priorities of the district. District leaders who help create the playbook better understand the strategies, as does everyone else who helps create the playbook, and they are better able to discuss instructional strategies with teachers as a part of instructional conversations.

OUR HOPE FOR THIS BOOK

The idea of an instructional playbook has caught fire since Jim described it in *The Impact Cycle* (2017). In schools, every day is "game day." Every day, teachers need the best resources and the best forms of support because students deserve the best we can offer them. The playbook aims to be that kind of support: the best strategies with the best research base that best target teachers' goals for students. We hope this book helps educators create playbooks that produce a common language about high-impact teaching strategies, deepen everyone's understanding of what instructional coaches do, and most importantly, support teachers and students in classrooms.

To guide you in using this book, the chapters are laid out in a consistent way:

 Each chapter begins with a **LEARNING MAP** depicting the key concepts in the chapter. We are visual people and we hope this is helpful to you.

Each chapter ends with these four reflective sections:

 TO SUM UP provides a summary of each chapter.

 MAKING IT REAL describes practical actions that educators can take to turn the ideas in each chapter into actions.

 REFLECTION QUESTIONS are intended to prompt readers to make connections and examine ideas about each chapter's content.

 GOING DEEPER introduces resources (mainly books) that readers can explore to extend their knowledge of the ideas and strategies in each chapter.

Throughout the book, you will also find the process for creating a playbook including checklists, playbook FAQs, and a curated selection of sample items from playbooks submitted to us by educators to consider when creating your own playbook.

MAKING IT REAL

Most creative acts are challenging, and to create something that is excellent, creators have to persist, push forward until what they create is beautiful or true, or, in the case of a playbook, simple, powerful, and very useful.

In *The War of Art* (2002), Steven Pressfield, an accomplished author who has become even more famous as a kind of creativity guru, argues that each of us carries within us a force that, if we let it, will hold us back and keep us from doing the work—the art—we are meant to do. Pressfield calls this force the Resistance. For Pressfield, the "war of art" is a battle between the voice inside of us that wants to hold us back and our creative genius, which holds the potential to move us forward.

This might seem a highfalutin way of thinking about creating an instructional playbook, but in our experience, when people work to create something as important and valuable as an instructional playbook, they are often tempted to give up before they get the kind of practical simplicity that they need. In developing the playbook, keep working until you have the tool you need. Then, and only then, will the playbook have the greatest impact.

TO SUM UP

An instructional playbook is a tool coaches can use to help teachers choose teaching strategies that help them hit their goals for students.

An instructional playbook consists of three components: (a) a Table of Contents that lists all of the strategies in the playbook; (b) a One-Pager of each strategy that explains its purpose, the research supporting it use, and how teachers and students use it; and (c) sufficient Checklists that help the coach to explain the key elements of the strategy and give the teacher a resource that supports them in classroom implementation of the strategy.

Creating an instructional playbook can involve coaches and other educators and is fundamentally an editing process to distill the most relevant, clearly explained, and high-impact strategies for teachers to use to hit goals for students.

The playbook is first and foremost a coaching tool to use in an Impact Cycle, but it can also serve as a tool for communicating what coaches do and what instructional coaching means for schools and school systems.

The Impact Cycle is a three-phase process for student growth. First, the coach assists the teacher in collecting data so that the teacher has a clear picture of classroom reality that enables setting a student-focused goal and selecting a teaching strategy (using the playbook) to use to hit that goal. The coach then ensures that the teacher understands the strategy deeply via checklists and modeling, and provides ongoing support (as requested by the teacher) until students hit the goal. Finally, coach and teacher draw on the playbook to make adaptations until the goal is met.

REFLECTION QUESTIONS

1. What was most valuable about this chapter?

2. What will your team need to do to overcome what Steven Pressfield refers to as "the Resistance," and create a great playbook?

3. In your mind, what will the perfect playbook look like?

4. What can a playbook accomplish for your school or district?

5. Which teaching strategies do you think are most important for inclusion in the playbook?

GOING DEEPER

The term "instructional coach" was popularized in articles written by Jim and in the first extended book on the topic, *Instructional Coaching: A Partnership Approach to Improving Instruction* (Knight, 2007), but definitions of the term abound. For more information on the research that Jim and his colleagues conducted to develop and validate instructional coaching, visit instructionalcoaching.com/research. You can also read *Instructional Coaching*, which examines why a partnership approach is more effective than a top-down approach, and *The Impact Cycle: What Instructional Coaches Should Do to Foster Powerful Improvements in Teaching* (Knight, 2017), which describes the Impact Cycle process in detail. *The Impact Cycle* also includes a complete instructional playbook in its toolkit. That toolkit is modeled on Jim's work on instruction in *High-Impact Instruction: A Framework for Great Teaching* (Knight, 2013), which presents 16 high-impact teaching strategies coaches can share with teachers, and includes checklists and videos to help coaches clearly explain strategies. We're biased, of course, but we think *High-Impact Instruction* is an essential resource for anybody developing instructional playbooks.

Bill Jensen's *Simplicity: The New Competitive Advantage in a World of More, Better, Faster* (2001) has been a huge influence on the thinking behind this book. Jensen's book is packed with wise and helpful ideas to help us live a simpler and better life, at work and at home. According to Jensen, finding simplicity is one of the most important leadership traits in complex times like ours.

"Most of us have two lives: the life we live and the unlived life within us. Between the two stands resistance."

//////////////

STEVEN PRESSFIELD

CHAPTER 2
CREATING THE TABLE OF CONTENTS

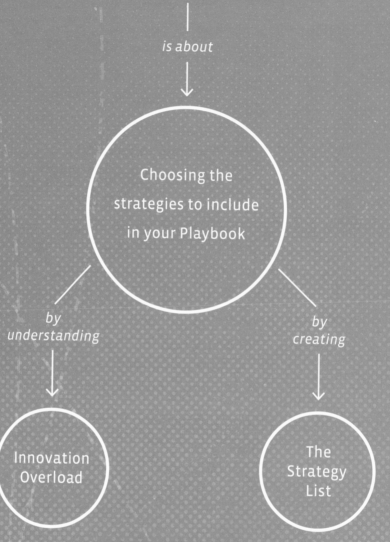

is about

Choosing the strategies to include in your Playbook

by understanding

by creating

Innovation Overload

The Strategy List

- impact blindness
- multiplier effects
- unfunded mandates
- band-aid initiatives
- cost myopia
- initiative inertia

- determine the audience, team members, and team boundaries
- determine common goals
- identify strategies
- reduce, refine, and organize the list

02

CREATING THE
TABLE OF CONTENTS

 SNAPSHOT:

This chapter describes how to go about identifying

the high-impact strategies to be included in your

Table of Contents. Also, the chapter describes a

process for creating your own list. You can skip

the chapter if you already know which teaching

strategies will be listed on your short list.

The art of being wise is the art of knowing what to overlook.

WILLIAM JAMES

Jim chose to become a professional developer for the reason most other educators do: He identified teaching strategies that made a difference for children and wanted others to learn what he had learned. In Jim's case, the strategies were part of the Strategic Instruction Model (SIM) developed at the University of Kansas Center for Research on Learning, where Jim has been a researcher since 1992. When he first learned about SIM (Deshler & Schumaker, 1988), SIM involved 12 learning strategies designed to help students improve how they read, write, and learn and another dozen content enhancement routines (Bulgren, Deshler, Lenz, 2007) designed to help teachers instruct in more inclusive ways. Each strategy and routine was described in an instructor's manual ranging in length from 75 to 125 pages or more, although some were hundreds of pages long.

To become a certified SIM professional developer, Jim had to create a portfolio of student work to demonstrate that he had taught the strategies effectively, and he read a large stack of research articles about SIM. Then he attended a week-long workshop as part of his certification process. After he was certified, armed with the hundreds of overhead transparencies he'd created, Jim started to conduct workshops at schools, colleges, and other organizations in Ontario, Canada, where he lived.

Right from the first workshop, Jim recognized he had some work to do as a professional developer. To prepare, rather than focusing on one or two of the teaching or learning strategies, he set out to learn everything at once, trying to read and remember hundreds of pages of text in the instructor's manuals and all the research he had read to become a certified SIM professional developer.

The result was not pretty. In trying to learn everything, Jim struggled to develop the deep knowledge he needed to be an effective professional developer. Despite his best intentions, on many occasions, he put a transparency on the overhead projector and then realized he could not remember any of the information he was supposed to share.

In his very first workshop on learning strategies, Jim shared a tsunami of overheads with little guidance on what to do with the information, so half-way through his session, the host of the workshop came to Jim and graciously said, "I think we've got a lot to think about. Maybe we should just stop right here, so all of us can take some time to think through what you have shared." Jim wanted to share everything he knew with his colleagues, but in trying to do everything, he came close to doing nothing at all.

Innovation Overload

What Jim's workshop participants experienced at the individual level has been experienced by many educators in schools or educational systems. In wanting to provide the best resources for their teachers and students, instructional decision-makers provide workshop after workshop on relevant topics. On occasion, the leaders' desire to meet the needs of all students ends up making it more difficult for teachers to learn important new teaching strategies.

For example, district leaders might want teachers to get a deeper understanding of their curriculum and, therefore, provide professional development in *Understanding by Design* (Wiggins & McTighe, 2005). They might also want teachers to be introduced to a wide range of powerful teaching strategies and, therefore, offer workshops in *High-Impact Instruction* (Knight, 2013) or *The Skillful Teacher* (Saphier, 2017). Then, to ensure that teachers understand the research behind certain practices, leaders might organize workshops on *Visible Learning* (Hattie, 2008) or *Classroom Instruction That Works* (Marzano, Pickering, & Pollock, 2001). Additionally, leaders might offer workshop on differentiated instruction (Tomlinson, 2014) or strategies for teaching students who are learning English (such as the SIOP model from the Center for Applied Linguistics; www.cal.org), or for culturally responsive teaching (Hammond, 2015).

With so many initiatives to consider—and all of them seemingly equally important—it is no wonder that teachers often become overwhelmed, experiencing a phenomenon known as "innovation overload." As Hollister and Watkins wrote in their 2018 *Harvard Business Review* article, "Too Many Projects," often "leaders keep layering on initiatives, which can lead to severe overload" (p. 3).

Although their research is conducted with businesses, Hollister's and Watkins' insights apply to many of the school districts we have visited over the past two decades. The following are some of the most relevant causes for innovation overload identified by the authors.

IMPACT BLINDNESS. Leaders in organizations "can be oblivious to the number and cumulative impact of the initiatives they have in progress" (Hollister & Watkins, p. 4). In schools, this may mean that leaders start initiatives without carefully weighing the demands that the initiatives might make on teachers, who already feel pressed for time. Teachers, faced with the overwhelming task of learning a new set of teaching strategies, may opt for the safest approach—to do the bare minimum.

MULTIPLIER EFFECTS. According to Hollister and Watkins, leaders often "have a line of sight into their own group's initiatives and priorities but a limited view of other groups' activities. Because... [groups]...often set their priorities and launch initiatives in isolation, they may not understand the impact on neighboring...[groups]" (p. 4). In schools, such a situation might arise when several divisions or groups within the district or building promote different initiatives without considering what other initiatives teachers might also need to learn. For example, if two initiatives are introduced each by language arts, mathematics, special education, technology, behavior specialists, and the superintendent, teachers may find themselves facing a dozen or more new programs to implement. For most of us, that is far too many to learn and use effectively.

UNFUNDED MANDATES. In business, Hollister and Watkins write, "executive teams often task their organizations with meeting important goals without giving managers and their teams the necessary resources to accomplish them" (p. 6). Much the same situation can arise in schools when, for example, instructional coaches are asked to do coaching but are not given sufficient time to coach, or when teachers are asked to lead professional learning communities but are not provided with additional time with those groups.

BAND-AID INITIATIVES. These kinds of initiatives refer to projects that only provide partial solutions to tough problems, resulting in "a proliferation of initiatives, none of which may adequately deal with root causes" (p. 7). In schools, this often involves a quick answer to an important challenge. For example, teachers who are struggling to meet the needs of students who are learning English might be given a two-day workshop on support for those students and no follow-up. As a result, teachers will struggle to implement the new strategies, and students don't get the learning support they deserve.

It isn't hard to see the attraction of band-aid solutions. Many school leaders face a large number of anxiety-inducing problems. Some students lack the learning strategies or basic skills they need to succeed. Others have special needs that the school has a moral obligation to address. Kids may lack motivation, need to learn self-regulation skills, or experience challenges outside of school. Faced with such wide-ranging issues, leaders understandably may be tempted to resort to anything that looks like it could at least be a partial solution. Admittedly, a quick fix can feel better than doing nothing, but in reality, quick fixes usually make the situation worse.

COST MYOPIA. One more quick fix that can increase overload is "cutting people without cutting the related work" (p. 7). This happens when organizations reduce the number of staff but don't decrease the amount of work everyone must perform without considering the related high price of employee burnout, performance strain, and turnover. Teachers might experience this when their class time is increased or their planning time is decreased. Similarly, coaches might experience this if they are expected to have a significant impact on student learning even though cuts to the numbers of coaches means they have impossibly high numbers of teachers to reach.

INITIATIVE INERTIA. Finally, the Hollister and Watkins write, "companies often lack the means (and the will) to stop existing initiatives" (p. 7). This happens in schools when redundant programs remain even though new programs are added. For example, a school might have several similar approaches to behavior management when one would be adequate, which leaves teachers, again, overwhelmed.

For all these reasons, we feel districts are wise to focus their attention on a few high-leverage strategies. Those strategies are described in a playbook, and creating the playbooks begins with creating the Table of Contents.

The Table of Contents

The Table of Contents is a single page that lists the teaching strategies that are included in the instructional playbook. We learned about the power of one-page documents from Bill Jensen's book, *Simplicity: The New Competitive Advantage in a World of More, Better, Faster* (2000). Jensen describes what he learned about one-page documents from Kent Greenes, CEO of a high-tech research and engineering firm. Greenes told Jensen, "we get people focused through one-page tools." Greenes went on, "if you can actually get everything on one page—and not just editing stuff out —that means the tool and process caused you to reflect on what it is you want to do ... If you limit the number of pages people have to explain themselves, it forces them to reflect first and think about what they're trying to do. That's very important" (pp. 52-53).

Limiting something to one page forces us to think and reflect deeply on the content. This means we need to know the most critical elements of the content and, as a result, we will most likely be better able to explain that content well and succinctly. That is, the coach therefore becomes a stronger coach in keeping these items to one page, just as the teacher becomes a stronger teacher as a result of the coach's clearer explanations.

To create a Table of Contents coaches must ask important questions about their roles, their coaching audience, and their system's role in the coaching process. Answering these questions leads to much greater clarity, as Dr. Karen Norris found when she created a playbook with coaches at Momentous Institute, a mental health agency that provides schooling services for clients in Texas, Tennessee, and Georgia. When we interviewed Dr. Norris, who coaches teachers as part of her work, she talked about how the playbook helped her team gain clarity:

What is it that we really want our teachers to know and be able to do? The playbook really [clarified] the work of our teachers here at Momentous, and clarified what we need to be coaching on, and how we need to be moving forward.

The Process

A story about Warren Buffett, one of the five richest people in the world, says a great deal about why the process of creating an instructional playbook is so important. The story goes that Mike Flint, Buffett's pilot for many years, once asked Mr. Buffett for advice on how to be more successful. Buffett gave him some simple advice: first make a list of the 25 things you want to accomplish. Then, go through the list and circle the five most important goals. After that, focus on the five most important things, and ignore the rest. The secret of success, then, according to one of the most financially successful people in the world, is focus.

The process of creating an instructional playbook is similar to the process Buffett recommends. We consider all the teaching strategies we could share with teachers to empower them to hit their goals, and then we narrow the list down to the most powerful and effective, ending with a one-page list of strategies that becomes the Table of Contents for the playbook. In short, the Table of Contents is a simple and powerful way to organize the playbook, focusing everyone on the most relevant, evidence-based teaching strategies so teachers and students can meet the goals set during coaching.

Creating the Table of Contents can seem like a daunting task. Instructional coaches are often charged with leading all kinds of professional development, so they typically know a lot about

"People think focus means saying yes to the thing you've got to focus on. But that's not what it means at all. It means saying no to the hundred other good ideas that there are. You have to pick carefully. I'm actually as proud of the things we haven't done as the things I have done. Innovation is saying no to 1,000 things."
///////////////,

STEVE JOBS

many different teaching strategies. When they start creating a playbook, coaches may feel as though they will never be able to synthesize all of that information on one page. At the same time, they may know that the strategies being used in a district are great matches for the goals most frequently set by teachers.

After coaching for a few years, many coaches discover that teachers consistently set similar goals, usually related to student achievement or engagement. The people creating the playbook should use those goals to identify the areas of focus for the instructional playbook to create a lean and clean document, and in this way, pull their school or district back from innovation overload. We like to say that it is better for coaches to know a few strategies well rather than to know a lot of strategies superficially.

Rachel LaForce, an instructional coach in Oklahoma City Public Schools, told us that creating an instructional playbook helped her feel more confident as she moved from being a pre-K teacher to working as a pre-K to grade 6 instructional coach. The playbook, she said, even helps her discuss learning outside of her coaching work. "Sometimes, when I'm having learning conversations, I'll say to myself, 'I have a strategy for that in my playbook.'" The learning that comes from creating a playbook can affect everyone.

We suggest teams move through five steps to create their Table of Contents: (a) determine the audience, team members, and team boundaries; (b) determine common goals; (c) identify strategies; and (d) reduce, refine, and organize the list.

CREATING THE TABLE OF CONTENTS

» Determine the audience, team members, and team boundaries.

» Determine common goals.

» Determine categories.

» Determine strategies.

» Continuous improvement.

DETERMINE THE AUDIENCE, TEAM MEMBERS, AND TEAM BOUNDARIES

CREATING THE TEAM. Determining the right number of people to create the playbook is an interesting challenge. The more people who are involved in creating the playbook, the more people end up with a deep understanding of the teaching strategies contained in it. Curriculum coordinators, school administrators, teachers, and school system leadership are all potential candidates for a team. Jana Claxton and Kristina Feldner, coaches in Irving Independent School District in Texas, felt it was important to "give voice and eyes to all areas" in developing their playbook to foster a shared understanding and common language.

While the inclusion of more people leads to more commitment and more understanding, involving more people slows down collaboration and decision making. As Jana and Kristina discovered, once the team began working on the playbook, members wanted to focus on their own, individual priorities and needed constant reminders to include only the strategies with the highest demonstrated impact on student learning and well-being. For this reason, the more people invited to the playbook sessions, the more important it is that group discussions be shaped by well-thought-out dialogue structures (see Knight, 2011, pp. 175-206). Ultimately, the make-up of the team should be determined by school leaders overseeing coaches in partnership with the coaches themselves.

One option adopted by some districts is to create two playbooks: a core playbook and a comprehensive playbook. The core playbook contains the essential strategies that people agree will be most helpful to students. Simply put, it contains the strategies that can be summarized on a Table of Contents, and is the version most often used by coaches who partner with teachers. The comprehensive playbook, on the other hand, contains all of the strategies that team members decided not to include on the Table of Contents. As such, it is a way of organizing other teaching strategies that remain a part of the overall professional development plan for a district, even though they are not at the heart of most coaching conversations.

A final point on team composition: We believe coaches must be at the heart of decision-making for the playbook. Coaches learn a lot about their collaborating teachers and are the people who most frequently help teachers implement the strategies that are in the playbook. The playbook is a coach's toolkit, designed to help coaches partner with teachers so teachers can have a more positive impact on students. As a result, coaches should have a significant voice in determining exactly what they will share with teachers.

Regardless of who participates in the process, the coaches we interviewed emphasized that working with others is important, that the task is too complex and the need for different perspectives is too crucial to "go it alone." Amber Thienel said, "You definitely need a team. I really wanted to do it by myself, just because I wanted to get it done, but there's no way! I could not have done this by myself at all. It's overwhelming on its own."

To determine the team composition and its members, the coach should ask the following questions:

DETERMINING THE PLAYBOOK TEAM

» Should coaches create a playbook with other coaches who have a role similar to theirs or with a variety of coaches with different roles?

» Should the team include specific curriculum coordinators who work closely with the coaching audience?

» Should the team include specific school administrators who supervise the coaching audience?

» Should the team include any specific teachers from the coaching audience?

» Should the team include any specific system administrators who supervise the coaching audience?

» Should the team include students or student voice in any way since students will be the ones experiencing the teaching strategies?

» Is there anyone else who should be a part of this process?

Every team will be different, uniquely shaped for the school or district where the playbook will be used, and only the particular roles that help shape a great playbook should be included. Everyone on the team should understand the reasons for creating the playbook and be committed to moving the process forward. In addition, the coach or coaches can decide if they want those broader perspectives involved for particular stages of the process or for the entire process. Keep in mind that, when others know more about the playbook, they will be better able to support coaches and better able to communicate about the playbook and coaching.

One final point: Diversity usually improves a team's creativity and effectiveness. As Steven Johnson explains in his book, *Farsighted: How We Make the Decisions That Matter the Most* (2018), "The connection between diversity and improvements in the collective IQ of a group has been demonstrated by hundreds of experiments over the past few decades" (p. 53). Johnson further notes that "a number of studies have shown that the addition of 'outsiders' to a homogenous group also helps the 'insider' come up with more nuanced and original insights on their own" (p. 53). A diverse team will create a better playbook.

AUDIENCE. Coaches' roles can be extraordinarily broad (e.g., elementary school generalist coaches who can coach any teacher on any goal), extraordinarily specific (e.g., behavior coaches who only work with teachers who teach students with behavior plans on their

"Some of the items that might be in our playbook came down from our coordinators and directors above us because they are initiatives that they want us using, but the biggest part of the playbook has come from us as coaches getting together and discussing and giving feedback to each other about what worked and what didn't. I would have to say that teachers probably have an indirect role in that because our feedback is based on the practice of what we find teachers are saying and doing in the actual coaching encounters."

//////////////

HARRISON MCCOY

*Instructional Content Coach
Education Service Center,
Region 11
White Settlement, Texas*

IEPs), or anywhere in between (e.g., mathematics coaches who may work across grade levels and content areas but only on goals involving mathematics). Determining the coaches' audience is a crucial first step in designing a Table of Contents that meets the needs of teachers and their students.

The team creating the Table of Contents should ask the following questions to the determine the coaching audience and characteristics:

» Do coaches focus on a specific group of teachers?
» Do all administrators and coaches agree on the coaching audience?
» Should coaches coach teachers who are not part of a coach's formal job description (e.g., special educators or resource teachers who work with teachers in specific content areas) and whose needs must be considered as well?

Once everyone is clear about the coaching audience, reaching out to other professionals who work with that audience is the next step.

STEP 2

DETERMINE COMMON GOAL AREAS

The kinds of goals teachers set during coaching has been an area of focus for our continuing research on instructional coaching. Initially, when studying coaching and goal setting, we tried to adapt the well-known SMART goals framework (Specific, Measurable, Attainable/Achievable, Realistic/Relevant, Time Bound) for *The Impact Cycle*, but we found that it was not a perfect fit. In particular, the "time bound" framework was challenging to implement given the complexity of teaching. That is, while we can use a time-bound goal to clean our closets using Marie Kondo's (2014) methods since we are the only person doing the cleaning, it is quite another thing to hit a goal related to students' emotional engagement with school.

To find a workable goal-setting framework, we considered several reviews of the literature on goal setting (Grant-Halvorson, 2012; Heath & Heath, 2010; Lopez, 2014) and found that other factors should be involved in creating effective goals. Ultimately, we created our own acronym related to goal setting, PEERS goals, described below.

PEERS GOALS

Student-focused goals must be:

» Powerful (for students)

» Easy (to understand and to communicate)

» Emotionally compelling (for the teacher)

» Reachable (measurable; strategy is identified)

» Student-focused (begin with "Students will ...")

POWERFUL. If teachers are going to invest time and emotional energy into hitting a goal, the goal needs to be worth the effort. The best goals have an unmistakably positive impact on student achievement and well-being.

EASY. When the teacher and coach have identified a powerful goal, they need to determine whether or not they have identified the simplest, clearest way to make a difference in children's lives. "Easy" does not mean watered-down, low-impact goals. In fact, the opposite is true. The best goals are both very powerful and very achievable, and since the goals occur within the complex setting of the classroom, there is no doubt that any powerful goal will inevitably involve some productive challenge.

EMOTIONALLY COMPELLING. As Heath and Heath wrote in *Switch: How to Change Things When Change Is Hard* (2010), the best goal is not "just big and compelling; it should hit you in the gut" (p. 76). Teachers who do not care about a goal usually have not set the goal themselves and likely won't reach the goal. However, teachers who decide which goals to hit, in partnership with the coach, generally care much more about goals.

REACHABLE. Reachable goals address the three elements of hope identified by Lopez (2014). First, they have a clearly stated, measurable goal, a finish line of sorts. Second, they include clearly stated pathways to a "preferred future" by identifying strategies that teachers can use to hit the goal. Finally, because they articulate a clear goal and pathways to the goal, they help teachers see that they can hit their goal and, therefore, increase teacher agency.

STUDENT-FOCUSED. Student-focused goals (i.e., they begin with "Students will...") answer the simple question, "Is this change making a difference?" In other words, if a teacher sets a goal of asking more open-ended questions (a teacher-focused goal), for example, that kind of goal has no measure of student impact built into it. On the other hand, if a teacher wants to increase students' cognitive engagement to 85% (a student-focused goal), then her goal will help her see if questioning is making a difference or if she has to try some other teaching strategy to meet the goal. This is one of our most important findings over the past decade. What matters is not the strategy that teachers use; what matters is the change in student learning or well-being. (See Knight, 2018, for more information on how to create measurable goals.)

The team facilitator should ensure that everyone understands PEERS goals before they start since the playbook's purpose is to catalogue and summarize the most powerful strategies coaches can share with teachers so that teachers and students can meet PEERS goals. Based on that understanding and agreement, the team can examine the most common coaching requests that coaches receive from teachers.

DETERMINING THE COMMON GOAL AREAS

- » Coaches bring individual data about coaching requests.
- » The team combines those requests into one list to determine the most common requests.
- » The team decides which request areas are the most relevant for the playbook.

Coaches need to bring data to the team meeting that summarize the coaching requests they receive and the goals they set with teachers. Coaches should present that information to start the conversation about goals. Once all of that information has been shared, the team should create a list of the goals that teachers most frequently identify during instructional coaching.

To ensure they come up with a comprehensive list, the team should discuss any new initiatives that are on the horizon (e.g., a new math curriculum, a perceived trend in student behaviors, a new system focus on students living in poverty) since the team may want the playbook to also address those issues. School and system administrators on the team can be especially helpful by alerting the team to new initiatives that may need consideration.

Finally, the team should edit and refine the list of goals to ensure that the list highlights the most frequent requests. Once the goals are stated and refined, the team can begin creating categories for the Table of Contents.

STEP 3
DETERMINE CATEGORIES

Although creating the categories for the Table of Contents can be a difficult, and sometimes even contentious, process, it is a vital part of playbook organization. After they have created categories, team members can check to make sure that their list addresses all the areas in which teachers request or need support. Additionally, a Table of Contents that is organized into categories is easier to understand, which makes it easier for coaches to explain what they do when they are introducing coaching to teachers who are new to the support they provide.

As with each stage of the process, this one also consists of three steps.

» The team brainstorms categories individually.

» The team brings together their suggestions to determine commonalities and differences.

» The team determines (perhaps with an affinity diagram process) which categories are the most relevant and appropriate for the playbook.

No one right way exists for organizing the Table of Contents into categories. Sometimes, system-wide priorities or very specific coaching roles suggest particular categories from the start of the process. We will describe two of those approaches, one based on using system-wide instructional frameworks to guide the process and one based on coaches who are tied to particular grade levels or content areas.

INSTRUCTIONAL FRAMEWORK APPROACH. School systems that use a particular instructional framework such as Hattie and Zierer's *10 Mindframes for Visible Learning: Teaching for Success* (2017) may decide that their Table of Contents should contain some elements of Hattie and Zierer's list.

» I am an evaluator of my impact on student learning.

» I see assessment as informing my impact and next steps.

» I collaborate with my peers and my students about my conceptions of progress and my impact.

» I am a change agent and believe all students can improve.

» I strive for challenge, not merely "doing your best."

» I give and help students understand feedback and I interpret and act on feedback given to me.

» I engage in as much dialogue as monologue.

» I explicitly inform students what successful impact looks like from the outset.

» I build relationships so that learning can occur in a place where it is safe to make mistakes and learn from others.

» I focus on learning and the language of learning.

The model playbook that Jim created for *The Impact Cycle* (Knight, 2017) uses fewer categories derived from his book on classroom instruction, *High-Impact Instruction:* Content Planning, Formative Assessment, Instruction, and Community Building (Knight, 2013).

Some school systems create their own instructional framework, bringing together strategies from many sources. For example, a district might combine Dylan Wiliam's and Siobhán Leahy's *Embedded Formative Assessment: Practical Techniques for K-12 Classrooms* (2015) with Carol Ann Tomlinson's *The Differentiated Classroom: Responding to the Needs of All Learners, 2nd Edition* (2014) and Randy Sprick's *CHAMPS: A Proactive and Positive Approach to Classroom Management* (2009) to create its own framework, and a district might organize a framework around categories suggested by those books. In some cases, playbook teams use the categories from *High-Impact Instruction* (Knight, 2013) (Content Planning, Formative Assessment, Instruction, and Community Building) even though their Table of Contents is not guided by that book.

CATEGORY LIST FROM HIGH-IMPACT INSTRUCTION

» Content Planning

» Formative Assessment

» Instruction

» Community Building

CONTENT-AREA APPROACH. For coaches with a very targeted coaching audience, creating initial categories may be fairly simple. For example, when Sharon became an instructional coach, her role was tied solely to high school English language arts, so her coaching audience was only English teachers and teachers in other content areas who wanted to use the reading, writing, speaking and listening, and language strategies that the English Department was implementing to meet the Common Core State Standards. She, therefore, organized her support around the four categories of those standards: reading, writing, speaking and listening, and language. Her role gave her a clear set of categories with which to begin.

In situations where coaching is focused on particular coaching audiences who have specific student-focused goals (e.g., only academic achievement, only behavior, only students with disabilities), specific categories are likely the best starting point. Other coaches may need to consider approaches that are broader and that involve a large array of goals.

PEDAGOGICAL APPROACH. Many school systems want their coaches to partner with teachers working in many content areas. This approach gives more teachers access to instructional coaching, but such a wide audience for coaching can make creating an instructional playbook a complex challenge.

Ann once worked with a group of more than 100 coaches, elementary, secondary, content area-specific, and not. To facilitate dialogue about the playbook, she shuffled the participants into groups of coaches with different roles across different grade levels and asked: "If you were suddenly asked to teach or coach in a very different setting (e.g., elementary instead secondary) or a completely new content area (e.g., social studies instead of math), which practices would you take with you to that new area?"

Ann's question led participants to identify categories that were broader and more about pedagogy (cooperative learning, formative assessment, student engagement), and all groups gained a broader understanding of the strategies coaches share with teachers. When different groups of educators collaborate across their groups, many benefit, especially educators who may not often have the opportunity to hear the perspectives from coaches in other contexts.

In summary, the most important thing is that educators choose the categories that make the most sense to them while recognizing that they can modify those categories over time as teacher or student needs change. Once the team has edited and refined the categories to accurately reflect the current needs of the coaching audience, they can begin designating specific strategies for each category.

DETERMINE STRATEGIES

Most educators find it difficult to identify the small number of essential teaching strategies that go on the Table of Contents. Educators love strategies. People who take on teacher support roles of any kind are, by and large, people who enjoy curriculum and instruction and lesson plans and experimentation, all of which involve instructional strategies. That is why when they hear the "one page and one page only" guideline for the Table of Contents, they think, "What? No way." This part of the process uses a three-step approach, but the process is deceptively simple because of how challenging the choices can be.

DETERMINING THE STRATEGIES

» Team members brainstorm strategies for each category individually.

» Team members bring together their suggestions to determine commonalities and differences.

» Team members determine (perhaps with an affinity diagram process) which strategies are the most relevant and appropriate for the playbook.

Making the best choices is challenging. Every strategy feels crucial, and every category for the Table of Contents feels imperative. But the truth is that if everything is a priority, then nothing is a priority. If everything is important, then nothing is important.

"Please don't hold any strategy in higher esteem than the learning of your students."
//////////////,
DOUG FISHER

There are many approaches to instructional problems and, as Michelle often says, they're all good, at least for some students in some situations. There are no bad strategies; a given strategy just may not be right for a given set of students. This begs the question, "Then how do I distill all of those wonderful strategies down to one page?" In the end, that problem is solved by research and by thinking in terms of strategies, not activities.

RESEARCH AND ITS LIMITATIONS. Research is important because it helps sort through which strategies, generally speaking, are most effective for increasing student achievement or well-being. A strategy that has a high effect size on Hattie's (2008) or Marzano's (2001) lists, for example, has a good chance of being more powerful than a strategy that has a low effect size.

Unfortunately, interpreting educational research is not a simple matter of picking the strategies at the top of a list. For example, researchers can arrive at conflicting findings. In the 2001 meta-analysis of instructional strategies, *Classroom Instruction That Works: Research-Based Strategies for Increasing Student Achievement* (Dean, Ross Hubbell, Pitler, & Stone, 2001), the authors grouped questioning together with advance organizers and cues and reported an effect size of 0.59. However, in the second edition of their book, they reported an effective size of only 0.20, but added that,

> Although the effect size for questioning was small
> among the studies that McREL researchers reviewed,
> other recent meta-analyses report large effect sizes
> that support the use of questioning as an instruc-
> tional strategy. Specifically, Schroeder, Scott, Tolson,
> Huang, and Lee (2007) found an effect size of 0.74
> for questioning in science, and Sencibaugh (2007)
> reported an effect size of 1.18 for questioning in
> reading comprehension. (p. 52)

Questioning, then, has an effect size somewhere between 0.20 and 1.18, and leaders may find themselves struggling to interpret the findings.

Another complication is the reality that although research findings present a synthesis of research, that research is necessarily general and does not always address the specific opportunities and challenges of individual classrooms. For example, some analyses of meta-analyses do not disaggregate data by socio-economic status or race. Also, many studies focus exclusively on achievement research, which means the analyses do not consider information on engagement, which is a major factor related to student dropout. Finally, general findings do not apply equally to all settings. For example, in Hattie's analysis time on task has a "respectable" effect size of 0.38, but most likely the effect size will be much higher in a classroom where a majority of students are not on task.

LOCAL EFFECTIVENESS. What, then, is an instructional leader to do? Of course, they should carefully consider research to identify the practices that will be used to help teachers hit their goals. At the same time, we suggest they also consider how well those teaching strategies help teachers actually hit their goals within their unique schools and classrooms. As such, we suggest that educators continually refine their Table of Contents so that it includes the strategies that are most effectively helping teachers hit their goals; that is, the strategies with local effectiveness.

Local effectiveness is our term for describing whether a teaching strategy helps individual teachers meet student-focused goals. Teaching strategies that are locally effective may not have high effect sizes, but they may prove over time to be powerful tools when used by individual teachers in particular systems. Local effectiveness can be determined by assessing whether teaching strategies enable teachers to hit goals. A strategy that helps teachers hit a goal stays in the playbook. Strategies that don't help teachers hit their goals are removed.

Leaders need to be careful about how they determine local effectiveness, however. A strategy shouldn't be kept because we have a hunch it will work. What matters is that the strategies enable teachers to hit clearly articulated, measurable, student-focused goals.

THE EMOTION FACTOR. Finally, the feelings people have about the teaching strategies they use can interfere with their ability to make decisions about what should or should not go on the Table of Contents. Indeed, when you listen to people talk about teaching strategies, you might hear them say, "I love that strategy," and when you love something, it is hard to take it off the list. For example, if a coach used a particular classroom management strategy for years when she was a teacher, she may want to include that strategy in the playbook even if another classroom management strategy has better research supporting its use. This is how creating the Table of Contents can become contentious: Team members may not only be debating the research merits of a particular strategy; they may also unknowingly make the coach feel as if they are telling her that she was wrong to have loved her strategy and wrong to have used it in the first place.

Once when Sharon facilitated an instructional playbook workshop, disagreements over strategies became so heated that a group of literacy coaches divided into two factions and refused to work with each other. The English language arts curriculum coordinator finally stepped in to broker a peace agreement between the two factions, but the feelings were intense, and the disagreements were significant. One might conclude that the coaches were over-reacting, but Sharon viewed it as evidence of how passionately teachers and coaches feel about strategies when they have had success with them in the classroom. When we believe that something works, it is not always easy to put it aside.

The only way around these emotional issues is for coaches to be candid about which strategies they have a bias for or against, and for everyone on the team to be clear about the kind of research support they want to follow in making choices (and, as with the literacy coaches mentioned above, perhaps to have an intermediary step in when choices become very tough). What matters most is selecting the strategies that will have the greatest impact on student growth. Coming back to that threshold again and again is the best way to make good choices.

STRATEGIES VS. ACTIVITIES. People developing a Table of Contents may also struggle if they are unclear about the difference between strategies and activities. As a working definition, we refer to "strategies" as categories of teaching practices and "activities" as individual examples of those strategies. For example, "cooperative learning" is a strategy that can involve many different activities. If those who are creating the Table of Contents want to include all of the more than 100 activities or learning structures from Kagan and Kagan's *Cooperative Learning* (2009) on their list, they will never fit that document on one page (Kagan and Kagan use three pages to list them). But if those developing the list simply use the term "cooperative learning," they leave themselves open to proposing any number of student activities to the teacher as part of cooperative learning if the teacher selects cooperative learning as the strategy.

For each strategy, coaches should ask each other, "Is this a strategy, or is it an activity that is part of a larger strategy or teaching practice?" Strategies and practices go on the list; activities do not. This process can feel ruthless and at times uncertain (especially because educators and researchers often do not define terms like "strategies" and "activities" the same way), but having the conversation around what works best for teachers is worth the challenge. (See the resources at the end of this chapter and CHAPTER 5 for samples of how coaches in various roles have selected strategies for their playbooks.)

CONTINUOUS IMPROVEMENT: THE PLAYBOOK SHOULD BE A LIVING DOCUMENT

Student needs change, and thus teacher needs change. Consequently, an effective playbook is a living document that responds to the dynamic nature of teaching and learning. By "living document," we mean that a playbook should be thoughtfully revised on a regular basis. Over time, as coaches work with teachers, they learn a lot about the teaching strategies they share. This learning may involve subtle refinements to checklists or greater recognition that particular strategies on the Table of Contents need to be replaced by other more effective strategies. As educators learn, their learning needs to be reflected in the playbook. Simply put, the playbook should contain all the important organizational learning about teaching and learning.

To ensure this happens, those who are developing the playbook should have a plan for thoughtfully reconsidering it on a regular basis, a plan for continuous improving it. Joi Lunsford in Amarillo, Texas, maintains her playbook in her Google Drive so that it is easy to revisit and update as teachers use the strategies and report back about how well they worked in hitting their goals for students.

> I have enjoyed the playbook being a living document and being able to value input from teachers, to just let them know again that they're the experts, they're the ones with kids, they're the ones implementing things. They are the ones doing that action research. We don't want to just put something on a piece of paper that sounds good in a perfect world. We want this to be real—powerful strategies that work with real students in a real classroom.

There are some simple steps a playbook team can take to establish a continuous improvement process. First, the team should set dates for when the playbook will be reviewed. We suggest these meetings happen at least three times a year. Second, the team should discuss what they have learned about teaching strategies. This should include what individual coaches have learned about improving individual checklists and what team members have learned about research or new strategies.

Third, the team should consider whether each strategy is proving to be locally effective. To that end, the team can ask a simple question: "Does the strategy enable teachers to hit the student-focused goals they are setting?"

Finally, the team should collectively discuss which changes should be made to the playbook. Instead of asking, "What works?," the team should use the threshold, "What works best?"

CONTINUOUS IMPROVEMENT

» Set dates when the playbook will be reviewed.

» Discuss what has been learned about teaching strategies.

» Review recent research in the area of concern to see if the strategy continues to meet the research requirements that the team has set.

» Examine each strategy for relevance. Ask, "Does the strategy meet the needs of the goals that teachers are setting?"

» Instead of asking, "What works?," use the threshold, "What works best?"

The group may also evaluate the strategies based on issues related to their specific context.

» Has the school or school system changed its instructional framework or key practices?

» Over the past year, have some of the strategies in the playbook not been chosen by any teachers for any goals? If so, those strategies may need to be removed.

» Do any new playbook team members have important contributions to make to the playbook?

» Is new information available on a specific strategy that may necessitate changes to the One-Pager for the strategy?

» Have teachers individually made changes to any of the checklists that may warrant changing the standard checklist for a given strategy?

All of these factors may result in revisions to the playbook. The most important part of continuous improvement is establishing a process in advance. Continuous improvement does not happen on its own. It requires a plan and a process.

When working with educators who are creating their playbooks, Michelle finds that she often needs to reassure them about the need to live with the ambiguity of a document that is never "finished." Finding peace with that element of the process is important because the "living" nature of the playbook is a reflection of its responsiveness to teacher needs, its respect for teacher choice and autonomy, and its emphasis on finding the best possible practices for teachers to use with students. Without continuous improvement, the playbook becomes just another instructional tome gathering dust in faculty bookrooms instead of the dynamic, relevant, and critical support it is intended to be.

MAKING IT REAL

To make this chapter real, get together with fellow coaches and/or other educators in your setting to discuss what your instructional playbook process might look like. Flesh out some specifics about what you all believe is the most efficient and helpful way to create a document that will be responsive to teacher concerns about their students.

TO SUM UP

Playbooks support teachers in hitting PEERS goals for students. Therefore, playbooks should reflect the goal areas that are most relevant to the teachers a coach supports.

Working together as a team to create a playbook is more manageable and effective than creating one alone. Coaches can decide which types of educators would be helpful on their playbook team.

Creating a Table of Contents involves three basic steps for each section of the document:

1. Coaches brainstorm the content for the section individually.

2. The playbook team comes together to sort, organize, and refine all that individual information.

3. The playbook team decides which pieces of the information are best suited to be included in the playbook.

Creating the Table of Contents is challenging because of the need to keep the document to one page and because of the emotional attachment that coaches often have to specific strategies.

Research can help educators choose effective teaching strategies, but the ultimate test of a strategy's power is its local effectiveness; that is, whether a strategy helps teachers and students meet goals.

Establishing a plan for continuously improving the playbook (making sure it is a living document) is crucial to keeping it relevant and helpful for teachers.

REFLECTION QUESTIONS

1. What was most valuable about this chapter?

2. Do you think you or your team should create a Table of Contents? Why? Why not?

3. If yes, what is your next step?

4. What resources (people, publications, websites, etc.) can you draw on to create a Table of Contents?

GOING DEEPER

Hollister's and Watkins' *Harvard Business Review* article "Too Many Projects" (2018) is a useful read for anyone interested in innovation overload, a phenomenon that is at odds with the purpose of an instructional playbook. Indeed, one of the most important reasons for creating a playbook is to reduce the endless lists of strategies teachers are to consider and instead to identify the strategies that have the highest impact.

Three books, in particular, have shaped our understanding of goal setting. Heidi Grant-Halvorson's *Nine Things Successful People Do Differently* (2012) is a concise and very useful book summarizing what research has to say about its topic. We suggest reading the digital version of the book if you're interested in the research, as each research article mentioned in the book is hyper-linked to the discussion.

Shane Lopez's *Making Hope Happen* (2014) is another favorite. Lopez explains hope's necessary elements, (a) a goal or preferred future, (b) pathways to the goal, and (c) agency, or a belief that the goal can be hit. We deeply miss Shane, who was a guide to so many researchers we have known. His work, however, still brings hope to thousands of people in the world every year.

CHAPTER 3
THE ONE-PAGER

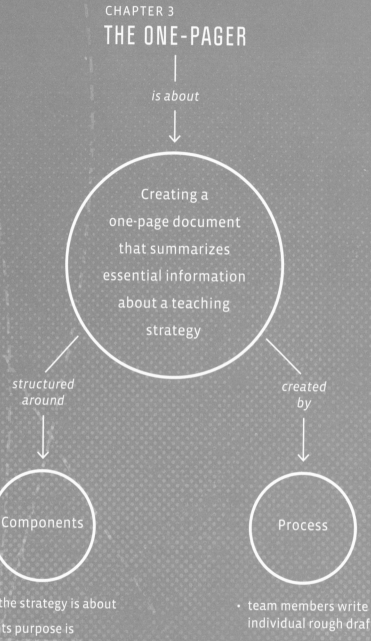

is about

Creating a one-page document that summarizes essential information about a teaching strategy

structured around

created by

Components

Process

- what the strategy is about
- what its purpose is
- the research that supports it
- how teachers use the strategy
- how students use the strategy

- team members write individual rough drafts
- group refines the documents
- share for feedback

03

THE ONE-PAGER

 SNAPSHOT:

This chapter describes how to create one-page summaries (One-Pagers) of the most important information related to the teaching strategies in the instructional playbook. The chapter also includes basic information about how to understand and consider research. You can skip this chapter if you are not going to create One-Pagers or if you are not interested in or already know a lot about research. If you are not sure if you will create One-Pagers, you could skim the chapter and then decide if you want to read it all.

The hardest work is figuring out what to
do in a world of infinite choices.

BILL JENSEN

Simplicity: The New Competitive Advantage in a World of More, Better, Faster

In Carol Reid's 1949 film-noir classic *The Third Man,* the main
protagonist, Holly Martins, a pulp fiction author, finds himself
wrapped up in a murder mystery in post-World War II Vienna.
The film is considered by many to be the greatest British movie
of all time, and in true film-noir style, it includes many dreamlike
or nightmarish scenes, with Mr. Martins running through the
post-war ruins or the catacomb-like sewers under the city.

For those of us who are coaches and professional developers,
however, the most nightmarish scene might be one that occurs
about a third of the way into film. Mr. Martins' stay in Vienna is
sponsored by a group who, after recognizing him as a writer, asks
him to give a talk to the local arts society on the modern novel.
Even though he knows little about the topic, short on cash, Martins
accepts the invitation because it will pay for his hotel room. Once
his bill is paid, he promptly forgets all about the talk.

At a later point in the film, Martins finds himself in a taxi racing
through the streets of Vienna toward a mysterious destination,
which turns out to be the meeting where he is to give the presenta-
tion he has completely forgotten about. Unprepared and with next
to no knowledge about at the topic (Martins says Zane Grey is his
greatest influence), the pulp fiction author stumbles through the
entire talk as, one-by-one, every member of the audience leaves,

heading out into the night to find something better to do. Finally, the room empty, the host of the meeting stands up and says to the empty room, "Ladies and gentlemen, if there are no more questions for Mr. Martins, I think I can call the meeting officially closed."

Our guess is that many coaches have had their own version of Holly Martins' experience in *The Third Man*. Many of us worry that we do not know enough about a given topic to share it with others or that we don't know the right information. Such worries are legitimate. Teachers will only be able to implement what coaches describe, and if coaches don't know or can't explain the most important elements of a strategy, effective implementation won't happen.

Further, even if we have deep knowledge of a particular teaching strategy, coaches may question whether they are qualified to talk about it. The well-known "imposter syndrome," first introduced by Pauline Case and Suzanne Immes in 1978, can lead coaches to wonder whether they should talk about teaching strategies at all.

When Jim asked coaches on Twitter how they experienced imposter syndrome, dozens replied. Dr. Sara Martens (@saramartens), for example, wrote, "I remember feeling like I had fooled people into hiring me," and Emily Roth (@EmilyRothie2) noted, "I used to experience imposter syndrome ALL the time as a coach." Tania Mansfield (@hktans) summed up what many coaches wrote on Twitter, "I feel I am so often faking it until I make it. Constantly doubting myself, my experience, and wondering, 'who am I to support and guide others in their journeys?'"

The imposter syndrome's widespread impact is also revealed in stories told by many incredibly successful people. Sheryl Sandberg, for example, CEO at Facebook and the best-selling author of *Lean In: Women, Work, and the Will to Lead* (2013), wrote about experiencing imposter syndrome:

Every time I was called on in class, I was sure that I was about to embarrass myself. Every time I took a test, I was sure that it had gone badly. And every time I didn't embarrass myself—or even excelled—I believed that I had fooled everyone yet again. One day soon, the jig would be up (p.28).

Similarly Neil Gaiman, who has won dozens of awards as a writer and creator, including the Newberry and Carnegie Medals, tells his own imposter syndrome story on his blog, journal.neilgaiman.com.

Some years ago, I was lucky enough to be invited to a gathering of great and good people: artists and scientists, writers and discoverers of things. And I felt that at any moment they would realise that I didn't qualify to be there, among these people who had really done things.

On my second or third night there, I was standing at the back of the hall, while a musical entertainment happened, and I started talking to a very nice, polite, elderly gentleman about several things, including our shared first name. And then he pointed to the hall of people, and said words to the effect of, "I just look at all these people, and I think, what the heck am I doing here? They've made amazing things. I just went where I was sent."

And I said, "Yes. But you were the first man on the moon. I think that counts for something."

And I felt a bit better. Because if Neil Armstrong felt like an imposter, maybe everyone did. Maybe there weren't any grown-ups, only people who had worked hard and also got lucky and were slightly out of their depth, all of us doing the best job we could, which is all we can really hope for.

To put imposter syndrome in perspective while also having the knowledge needed to effectively describe teaching strategies, coaches need tools that help them organize and communicate their knowledge about strategies. Those tools are the One-Pager described in this chapter and the Checklists described in CHAPTER 4.

What Is a One-Pager?

A One-Pager is, as its name suggests, is a one-page document that summarizes essential information about a teaching strategy. Once completed, the One-Pager functions as a concise communication tool coaches can share with teachers and others.

We've provided a sample One-Pager on the following page.

Sample One-Pager: Learning Maps

IN ONE SENTENCE:

A learning map is a graphic organizer depicting the essential knowledge, skills, and big ideas students are expected to learn in a unit, and is used to organize students' learning and teachers' instruction.

WHAT THE RESEARCH SAYS:

» According to Hattie's *Visible Learning* (2008), Student Expectations 1.44; Teacher Clarity 0.75; Concept Mapping 0.75.

» Students can use learning maps to review, monitor their learning, and confirm understanding.

» Learning maps are a form of concept map that teachers can use to ensure their lessons are clear.

WHAT'S THE POINT?

» Learning maps are powerful because their visual depiction of a unit keeps students and teachers on track.

» Learning maps are accommodations for students who struggle to take notes and structure the beginning and ending of lessons.

» Learning maps are living study guides that make connections explicit and support repeated review.

HOW ARE LEARNING MAPS USED BY TEACHERS?

» Teachers should spend 25-40 minutes to introduce the unit through an interactive discussion of the map on the first day of a unit.

» Throughout the unit, the maps may be used as visual prompts for conversations around advance and post organizers.

» Teachers should prompt students to record new information on their maps as it is learned.

» At the end of the unit, maps can be integrated into the unit review.

HOW ARE LEARNING MAPS USED BY STUDENTS?

Students use learning maps:

» to take note of key information,

» to frequently review and clarify their learning, and

» as points of departure for classroom dialogue.

While any playbook design team should structure their One-Pager in whatever way works best for their district or school, we have found that a simple structure works best for us.

First, the One-Pager starts with a one-sentence statement that concisely and expressively summarizes what the strategy is about. Anybody who reads the one-sentence summary should understand the core idea and value of the teaching strategy it describes.

Second, the One-Pager includes a summary of some of the most relevant educational research related to the strategy. This often involves making a connection to Hattie's (2008) or Marzano's (2017) analyses along with other relevant studies.

Third, the One-Pager includes a summary of the main reasons why people might use a given strategy—that is, an explanation of the purpose of the strategy; a description of how teachers use the strategy; and a description of how students use the strategy. Often, these descriptions take the form of bullet lists to make them more concise and easier to understand.

THE COMPONENTS OF A ONE-PAGER

An explanation—in the briefest terms and with the greatest precision—that includes

» what the strategy is about

» what its purpose is

» the research that supports it

» how teachers use it

» how students use it

The Purpose of the One-Pager

One-Pagers serve two important purposes: deepening coach knowledge and serving as a communication tool.

DEEPENING COACHING KNOWLEDGE

Distilling all of the information about a teaching practice onto one page is, like explanation itself, a focused, creative, and intellectual task. It requires investigating the research on a particular practice and considering the strategy's purpose, its use with teachers, and its impact on students.

Simple explanations are deceptively complex. Surprisingly, when we know something very well, we often find it difficult to explain it well to others. Without realizing it, we can assume more prior knowledge and understanding on the part of the listener than he or she might have, which causes our descriptions to be superficial or unclear.

Sometimes our explanations fail because

» we include too much detail,
» we don't stop to check for understanding,
» we unintentionally leave out pieces of information when describing concepts that we know well, or
» we try to describe so many elements of a complex task that most people struggle to remember it

The One-Pager requires explaining—in the briefest terms and with the greatest precision—what the strategy is about, what its purpose is, the research that supports it, and how teachers and students use it. When creating a document that summarizes all of that information about a teaching strategy on one page, coaches need to understand the strategy deeply, and the resulting document helps everyone else understand each strategy more easily. Maureen Hill, an instructional coach in Wilmington, North Carolina, says, "The playbook itself—just working on it, just trying to develop my own one-page sheet, my own checklists—really makes me be clear and concise, and I struggle with that."

Putting together the One-Pager is further complicated by each coach's own experience with a given strategy if they used it when they were teachers. Coaches have told us during research interviews that when they have a great deal of experience with a particular strategy, they have to resist telling teachers to use it exactly the way they used it themselves. The more attached a coach is to a strategy, the more challenging partnership can become. Additionally, while wading through the research, the coach may discover that he or she has not used the strategy for its intended purpose or has modified it in ways that are not aligned with the research and, as a result, feel incompetent to share the practice with others.

The first schoolwide professional development session Sharon ever attended was based on Carol Ann Tomlinson's work, *The Differentiated Classroom* (1999). Sharon loves lesson planning and immediately began modifying her lessons according to content, process, and product in the manner she thought that Tomlinson had specified, and she even received praise from school leaders in her efforts. But over the years, she wondered why those modifications did not have the intended effect on students, unaware that she was merely making modifications to plans without deeply examining them for their connections to the standards or to specific student needs, or with a critical eye toward rigorousness.

Years later, when Sharon attended a session led by a differentiation expert at a national conference, the presenter humorously opened the morning by thanking everyone for wanting to meet individual needs: "I'm grateful for that and that you want to differentiate instruction for students. But I'm here because, well, you're all doing it wrong." The presenter spent the next hour explaining what she meant. She was right: Sharon was doing it wrong.

After Sharon first became an instructional coach, requests for help with differentiation terrified her. She had worked to improve in that area over the years (including deep work with an instructional coach), but the voice in her head remained, "Differentiation: I do that wrong." How could she help other teachers when she had not aced the topic in her own classroom? She did not fully understand then the power and helpfulness of the coach as a learner, a learner who "dives deep" into a strategy to understand thoroughly what she doesn't know to more ably assist teachers.

Rachel LeForce, an instructional coach in Oklahoma City Public Schools, had a similar experience. When she first became an instructional coach, she was concerned about coaching teachers in grade levels with which she had limited experience. "I work in a building where I serve pre-K through sixth grade, so I have really had to stretch myself. Putting together this playbook and using it as a tool helped me become more competent in strategies that might be more relevant to grade levels I am not quite as comfortable with."

Rachel's inexperience might have helped her create a better playbook because she didn't make assumptions about her knowledge and consequently was more open to the learning that resulted from deep exploration of the practices. In short, the playbook can inform the coach's professional learning needs as much as it supports the teacher's.

The playbook provides thoroughly vetted, high-impact strategies in a lean and clean menu that coaches can share with others so that they can quickly understand the strategies and choose the strategies they will use to try and hit their goals. The playbook is not a compendium of everything that a coach knows about instruction. In fact, maintaining an openness to understanding what one does not know can be a benefit for coaches in creating the One-Pager.

SERVES AS A COMMUNICATION TOOL

A major goal of the One-Pager is clear communication. Keeping the One-Pager short forces us to develop the deep knowledge needed for clear explanations. In some situations, in fact, the depth of knowledge that is produced by the One-Pager makes it easier for a coach to explain strategies to help teachers choose a strategy to hit a goal.

"I didn't have time to write a short letter, so I wrote a long one instead."

//////////////

ATTRIBUTED TO MARK TWAIN

For some teachers, the prospect of selecting a teaching strategy to use to accomplish a PEERS goal can feel overwhelming. "If I knew what to do," a teacher may say, "I'd already be doing it." Sometimes coaches, too, are at a loss to think of a strategy on the spot or unsure about what to say about a strategy to help the teacher make a wise choice about what strategy to try.

When the coach uses the playbook in that goal-setting discussion, the elements of the One-Pager become key talking points for the teacher and the coach. If she thinks it can help, the coach can use the information on the One-Pager for each of the available strategy choices for the goal and then discuss those options with the teacher. For example, the teacher may want more clarity on the research studies supporting a given strategy's use, or the coach may need to provide more detail about the students who will be using the strategy. In some cases, none of the choices may appeal to the teacher, and the coach can then say, "I'll find you more options."

What matters most is that the teacher is the decision maker. The coach shares high-impact teaching strategies with the teacher and is ready to find more options as necessary. The entire exchange is grounded in dialogue, reflection, and learning that serve students.

THE ONE-PAGER SERVES TWO PURPOSES:

» A concise summary of the most important information about a teaching strategy

» A power tool for teachers deciding which strategy to use to hit a goal

THE POWER OF EVIDENCE

Joel Beyenhof, a high school principal in Council Bluffs, Iowa, partnered with his instructional coaches to create their school's instructional playbook. He believes his team's focus on research during the creation of the playbook helped the coaches offer better strategy choices and helped teachers make better decisions about which strategies to use with students.

When we interviewed Joel, he told us, "Sometimes teachers hear about a new strategy and think it's the best fit for them because they read an article about it, or it's trendy. Sometimes coaches are more comfortable from their own experiences with a certain array of strategies, but that might not mean that the strategy is a good fit for the students or teachers in a particular classroom."

"With the instructional playbook," Joel says, "We want our teachers to have a way of thinking that's formative in nature, and they approach that in a learning stance of, 'How do the choices and actions I take get students to the desired outcomes?' That way, we don't just measure progress in the sense of the teacher being masterful at executing a strategy. We measure progress in terms of how students are performing: 'If the students are not all performing at the level you want them to, what changes in the strategy would you make?'"

Because coaches ensure that each choice in the playbook has clearly demonstrated its effect on students, the educators in a school can have a great deal of confidence that teachers are implementing best practices that are targeted to specific student needs. As Dr. Karen Norris, from Momentous Institute says, "The buck stops with the practices that are most impactful for student learning." When a school faculty engages in the most powerful practices available, the school becomes a rich environment for powerful learning and growth for students.

THE POWER OF PARTNERSHIP

A major finding of our research is that coaching should be conducted as a partnership (Knight, 1999). Coaching is a conversation between peers, a dialogical, equal conversation where everyone's voice is heard and everyone's ideas shape the outcomes. Our research, along with a large body of other research including Deci and Ryan (2000), shows that partnership increases teachers' commitment to learning and implementing new strategies. Telling professionals what to do is a poor strategy for change because it decreases motivation and commitment and because it is a disempowering approach that fails to tap into all that teachers already know. Simply put, to treat teachers as professionals, we must treat them as partners.

When we create a document such as an instructional playbook, we may be tempted to share it in a top-down way. But when doing so, the playbook may come to be perceived as a school's or a system's "user's guide" of required teaching practices. Administrators with the best intentions may create a "learning walk checklist" out of the Table of Contents, which can cause teachers to see the playbook as yet another evaluation tool, yet another "hammer" in a model of perceived rewards and punishments. Too often school systems operate with top-down structures that are so entrenched that they may be invisible to teachers but still feel punitive. The playbook should not become another intervention foisted on teachers that gives them no voice in implementation.

Working in such top-down environments, coaches often are tempted to become directive as well. As Michael Bungay Stanier explains (2016), "Our brains are wired to have a strong preference for clarity and certainty, it's no wonder that we like to give advice. Even it if it is the wrong advice—and it often is—giving it feels more comfortable that the ambiguity of asking a question" (p. 60). Stanier refers to this urge to advise as the "advice monster":

> You have the best of intentions to stay curious and ask a few good questions. But in the moment, just as you are moving to that better way of working, the Advice Monster leaps out of the darkness and hijacks the conversation. Before you realize what's happening, your mind is turned towards finding The Answer and you're leaping in to offer ideas, suggestions, and recommended ways forward. (p. 60)

In wanting to help teachers, coaches may end up advising more than listening. Unfortunately, when we give advice that has not been requested, the unstated message is, "I don't think you can solve this issue on your own." For this reason, coaches should share the playbook as a menu of options rather than as a prescription. As Amber

Tell less and ask more
Your advice is not as good
As you think it is
////////////////,
MICHAEL BUNGAY STANIER

Thienel states, "The biggest challenge is just taking ourselves out of it. We know which direction that we'd want to go in, but who are we to say that this is the best direction for the teacher to take? We want the teacher to have more choice in the direction they want to take."

To prevent the playbook from becoming a disempowering, top-down tool, coaches must ensure that teachers make the final decisions about the goals they want to hit and the strategies they want to use. When teachers make their own choices about their classrooms, they are committed learners. When they are expected to do what they are told, they lose motivation, shifting from being committed to being compliant—perhaps even resistant. We want teachers who are empowered and excited about implementing new teaching strategies, not teachers who passively say, "Just tell me what to do, and I'll do it."

When partnership is the foundation of the process, change happens. Michele Kavars, a gifted strategist for the Multi-Tiered System of Support in Iowa, says that the playbook has engaged teachers more deeply in new practices: "I'm really seeing a much greater level of implementation than if we had an article or book study."

She believes that is "because the playbook represents instructional choices they can make. It's not me coming in and dictating what we're going to do." Hilary Herrmann, professional learning coordinator for Poudre School District in Ft. Collins, Colorado, agrees: "The playbook gives the teachers agency. It has helped the coaches internalize the lesson of not just telling teachers what to do." Partnership and autonomy are crucial in shifts in instruction.

Giving teachers more control and decision-making choices can be challenging for some, especially in places where partnership is not the norm. To determine how much autonomy teachers may need, leaders need to ask themselves, "Is our professional development working?" If not, giving teachers more responsible autonomy can be a way through. We all want teachers to believe in the capability and promise of each student, so leaders must also ask themselves, "Do I believe in the capability and promise of each teacher as well?" As Joel Beyenhof, explains, "If you approach people as if they don't know what they're doing and don't have the capacity, then all you're going to have are some well-designed documents that don't really lead to change." We believe in meaningful change and in teachers, so we believe in partnership.

The temptation to adopt a top-down approach to change is understandable since everyone wants better outcomes for kids, and the seemingly easiest approach is to just tell teachers what to do. But more than 30 years of research by Edward Deci, Richard Ryan, Teresa Amabile, and others shows control does not work. Just telling teachers what to do creates dependence, which is why so many teachers who are not used to having a sense of autonomy say to coaches, "Just tell me what to do."

Taking autonomy from teachers communicates that leaders don't trust teachers to think for themselves. With regard to the instructional playbook, there is a paradox at work. We want the teacher to be the decision maker, but we want the playbook to be clear and precise. Both are essential. If coaching is about "unleashing the potential," as coaching pioneer Sir John Whitmore says, then leaders need to communicate that they believe in their teachers' potential.

As teachers wrestle with the One-Pager strategy choices, coaches should structure conversations so that teachers feel free to ask questions, challenge assumptions, and ask for more choices. The more confident teachers feel about their choices, the more deeply they will engage in implementation that positively affects students.

To build One-Pagers that provide the best choices, we will now focus on how to evaluate research and the steps involved for each of the five sections of the page.

Research and the One-Pager

An important part of the One-Pager is the research section. Research is important because it provides an objective way of determining whether a teaching strategy or other intervention, such as coaching, will work in a particular environment. For example, research can help us better understand if teaching strategies used by a teacher, school, district, or state will have a positive impact on students' learning or well-being.

In the section below, we identify questions that anyone can ask to think deeper about educational research. These questions provide a quick overview, and if you already have a deep knowledge of educational research, you might choose to skip this section.

QUANTITATIVE RESEARCH

We believe that neither quantitative nor qualitative research is superior to the other, but that the two approaches serve different purposes. When we look at a study, therefore, we recognize that the findings should be read differently depending on what kind of study it is. Quantitative research currently has the most influence on the decisions made about teaching practices or approaches to coaching, so we will start there.

When researchers conduct quantitative research, they use numbers to support their findings. Usually, this involves controlled experimental design. For controlled experiments in schools, people are randomly assigned into two groups. One group then gets a "treatment" (an intervention of some kind), while the other does not get the treatment but usually gets some alternative treatment. Often the non-treatment group gets a placebo, something that appears to be an intervention but actually shouldn't have any impact. Then scientists measure impact by comparing the outcomes of the two groups.

Two factors come into play here. The dependent variable is the thing that is measured. The independent variable is the thing that is manipulated. Thus, if we are conducting a scientific study to determine whether or not a diet pill makes any difference, the independent variable would be the diet pill. The dependent variable would be the possibly changing weight of each of the research participants.

IS THE RESEARCH EVIDENCE-BASED?

When Jim and other researches were conducting interviews with coaches, teachers, and administrators for *Focus on Teaching* (Knight, 2014), one theme that came up repeatedly was that most people do not have a clear picture of what it looks like when they do what they do, a finding that is also a part of the literature on the personal experience of change (Prochaska, Norcross, & DiClemente, 1994). Because of perceptual errors such as confirmation bias, habituation, stereotyping, recency effect, and primacy effect, most people experience a very distorted version of reality. As a famous quotation states, "We don't see things as they are; we see them as we are."

Research can help us be more objective in our discernment. One way we sometimes describe using research in this way is to talk about evidence-based practices. We say something such as a teaching strategy is evidence-based when researchers share findings—whether their own of somebody else's—that suggest something is effective, or works. Sometimes the label of "evidence-based" indicates that while specific elements of a practice or approach are supported by previous research, modified practices or approaches may not have been fully tested by researchers. Understanding the extent to which a practice has been studied (either in part or as a whole) is key to knowing what kind of predictions we can make about its use in specific classrooms.

WAS THE RESEARCH PEER-REVIEWED?

People, including researchers, tend to like the things they create. So researchers need to have checks and balances in place to attempt to keep bias out of their study and ensure that they are truly being scientific. A major way to counteract bias in research is through peer review.

Peer review means that other researchers analyze and critique a study before it is published, determining whether or not it is rigorous enough to be published or presented. Peer-reviewed journals are publications that only accept research studies after they have gone through peer review. Peer review is also a requirement for studies to be presented at research conferences such as the American Educational Research Association Conference. Studies that have not undergone peer review are at risk of reflecting a researcher's bias and, therefore, should be read and interpreted with care.

ARE THE FINDINGS SIGNIFICANT?

To demonstrate the answer to a research question, researchers need to show statistical significance. Statisticians perform various types of statistical analyses to show that a change in the dependent variable is because of the independent variable, and not because of chance or error. When research shows a statistically significant change, we assume it is because of whatever is being studied.

DOES THE RESEARCH HAVE ECOLOGICAL VALIDITY?

Just because a study shows significant impact in clinical settings does not mean that it will work in typical classrooms. For example, teaching strategies that are taught in small groups in clinical settings might not work in regular classroom settings. Research should show ecological validity (it clearly states the environment in which it has demonstrated evidence of effectiveness). And that's why, when analyzing studies, educators need to ask and study, "Will this work in my setting?" That is another reason why an instructional playbook must be a living document. We need to test out the teaching strategies, keep and refine what works, and delete what doesn't work. Over time, with revision, the playbook should become a more and more powerful tool for the teaching practices that teachers choose.

IS THERE A LARGE EFFECT SIZE?

The greater the effect size, generally speaking, the greater the positive impact on student achievement. Effect size is calculated by comparing the averages of two different results. In educational research, that comparison is often between the average score of an experimental group and the average score of a comparison group. Or as Robert Coe has written (2002), "Effect size is just the standardized mean difference between two groups" (p. 3).

DETERMINING EFFECT SIZE:

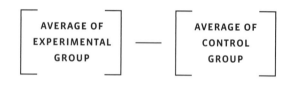

$$\frac{\text{AVERAGE OF EXPERIMENTAL GROUP} - \text{AVERAGE OF CONTROL GROUP}}{\text{THE SPREAD FROM THE MEAN (STANDARD DEVIATION) OF THE CONTROL GROUP}}$$

John Hattie's work has popularized the importance of effect size. He and Klaus Zierer have written the following: "The beauty of effect sizes is that, once computed, they can be reasonably compared across many interventions" (Hattie & Zierer, 2017, p. ix).

Hattie's work analyzes meta-analyses. A meta-analysis combines the average effect sizes of a strategy or intervention across multiple studies. Because a meta-analysis involves more than one study, it is considered more powerful evidence of effectiveness than one study. Nevertheless, a few questions should be considered when reading meta-analyses.

First, we must ask, "What if individual studies have larger effect sizes than those calculated for meta-analyses?" For example, Johnson and Johnson's research on cooperative learning (2013) shows an effect size of .71, but in Hattie's meta-analysis (2018), cooperative learning is listed as having different effect size of .59. Does that mean that Johnson and Johnson are wrong, or does it mean that people who want to do cooperative learning should do it as spelled out by Johnson and Johnson?

Second, when we analyze effect size, we need to ask, "What is being measured?" A large effect size for achievement, for example, might not be the most important statistic if we are concerned about student dropout, where student engagement might be more important.

Third, effect size is historical, which means it only summarizes what has been studied in the past. It doesn't include what is new. For that reason, we should ask, "Do the challenges we face in schools need strategies that are innovative even though they lack significant data in their support?"

The answer to each of the above questions does not have to be yes or no for a given strategy to be effective in a given situation. Indeed, some studies that are not backed by a lot of evidence may still be powerful in individual classrooms. Telling stories, for example, is a teaching strategy we recommend even though it is not mentioned in either Hattie or Marzano's work. And some strategies with a relatively low overall effect size might still be uniquely powerful in particular classrooms or schools. What matters most is whether a strategy increases student learning or well-being. That is why we suggest that a playbook should be a living document, shaped by what is learned locally about how effectively a strategy works in each classroom, school, or district.

IS IT QUALITATIVE RESEARCH?

Some aspects of what happens in schools are better studied through qualitative rather than quantitative research. Qualitative research is used to understand the complex dynamics of individuals, organizations, and cultures. When researchers conduct qualitative research, they use research to gather and tell the stories of individuals and groups.

One example of qualitative research is naturalistic inquiry (Lincoln & Guba, 1985), a methodology we have used on several occasions. For example, we used naturalistic inquiry in 2006 to identify the characteristics of highly effective coaches. Our study involved two site visits to Florida where, at the time, 2,600 coaches were working within the Just Read Florida initiative across the state. For our first site visit, we met with 35 coaching supervisors to identify key attributes of effective coaches. The supervisors, in turn, identified 35 outstanding coaches; we narrowed that group to 5 coaches who represented a diverse sample of coaches in the state. Then our research team of 9 people went to Florida to interview the coaches, principals, teachers, and coaching supervisors who worked with the 5 highly effective coaches.

Following this, all interviews were transcribed and loaded into a qualitative research software program and analyzed. The analysis involved unitizing, categorizing, filling in patterns, and developing a narrative report. For example, one category consisted of all the units of information about how coaches communicated with teachers. The information was reviewed by researchers until themes and subthemes emerged. To make sure that our findings were accurate, we shared our research with coaches and made some revisions based on their feedback. The results of the study were eventually presented at the annual meeting of the American Educational Research Association (Knight, Cornett, Skrtic, Kennedy, Novosel, & Mitchell, 2010).

Although naturalistic inquiry is a major methodology within qualitative research, there are many others, including ethnography and case study. Two approaches that we feel have great potential for studying coaching are grounded theory (Brené Brown's chosen methodology) and portraiture, described by Lightfoot and Hoffman Davis (1997).

The knowledge generated by qualitative research is used differently than the knowledge generated by quantitative research. With quantitative research, the idea is that, if the sample is big enough, we can feel confident that what the research study shows will apply to our own lives (or, in the case of education research, to our students). With qualitative research, we take knowledge that is surfaced in a less direct way, and apply it to our work or lives in the same way we might apply a story to our work or to our lives. Stories can give us validation, warnings, advice, and inspiration, but not every story we hear will tell us what we need to do to get better.

Creating the One-Pager

Everyone who creates One-Pagers for the strategies in their playbook is writing their own creative document, so they are free to do it in the way that works best for their teachers and students. This means that people may choose to skip the research section or include sections that are not described here to create the best possible document for their school or district.

However, if you include a research section, you do so to show the power of the strategies in your playbook. If we can say that formative assessment has an effect size of .70 in Black and Wiliam's (2005) meta-analysis and a .90 effect size in John Hattie's research (2016) (where he refers to it as "formative evaluation"), then we are giving teachers significant evidence to suggest that formative assessment is important.

Ultimately, a high effect size need not and should not be the only way to validate a teaching strategy. As mentioned throughout, what matters most is that the strategies help students hit achievement or engagement goals. When teachers set goals with coaches, coaches help teachers implement strategies for those goals, and the strategies help teachers and students hit goals, then we can say a given strategy works. Impact, ultimately, determines whether a strategy is helping teachers to have a positive impact on student learning and well-being. For this reason, coaches and other educators who are involved in creating the playbook should continually revise it based on what is most effective in helping teachers and students hit goals.

CREATING THE ONE-PAGER

One way to understand the importance of the One-Pager is to consider an old hobby of Jim's. For many years, Jim would trade live recordings of concerts with other music lovers he met on the Internet. For example, Jim might send a recording of Jerry Garcia and David Grissman to someone in Telluride, Colorado, in exchange for a copy of Neil Young and Joni Mitchell giving a concert together.

Jim learned quickly that the more times a recording has been recorded, the less sharp it is. So if he got a recording that had been re-recorded many times, it did not sound too great since, with each recording, the tape had grown noisier and duller. The best tapes were the clean, high-fidelity, first-generation recordings.

Often a teacher's first exposure to teaching practices is a bit like Jim's experience with an eighth-generation recording of Dylan and the Band at London's Albert Hall. Teachers often learn about strategies from colleagues who may have heard it from someone else. The person explaining the strategy is not the creator, and he or she may have heard from someone else, who, in turn, learned about it from someone else. Our colleague tells us that the strategy is research-based, effective, and suited to our students. He or she tells what the strategy looks like, what resources we need to use to implement it, and how students should improve when using it. But just as in the case with Jim's old recordings of the Grateful Dead, with each generation, that is, each time someone describes the strategy to someone else, quality may be lost, and the strategy may become less effective with each explanation.

The act of creating the One-Pager takes educators back to the source and causes them to examine everything about each teaching strategy carefully to understand it more deeply. The authors of the playbook should consider questions such as:

» Where did this strategy come from?
» Which student populations should use it?
» What is it designed to do?
» What should it look like?
» How will I know it's working?

Answering these questions deepens and broadens everyone's understanding of the strategies in the playbook.

THE PROCESS

The playbook should increase teachers' capacity to choose the best possible strategy because it provides them with solid classroom teaching practices to consider as they seek out ways to hit the goals they have set for their students. The One-Pager summarizes the most important information about those practices, so capturing the information for it is fundamentally an editing process. Working to view the One-Pager through teachers' eyes can be helpful as well. Maureen Hill, an instructional coach at Murrayville Elementary in Wilmington, NC, sees the One-Pager as important in navigating teachers' uncertainty: "I think that often

> *"I love coaching because it's meaningful professional development based on what the teacher feels like they need at that moment. They aren't sitting in a training that they aren't sure they need or that they may or may not feel is something that's applicable for them."*
>
> ////////////////,
>
> **JOI LUNSFORD**
>
> *PLC and Teacher Support Instructional Coach, Canyon Schools, Amarillo, Texas*

they don't know which strategy to use, so having that one-page sheet for them to look over a few strategies and say, 'Oh, that's what I want to do,' has been a helpful tool."

When Ann guides teams to create their One-Pagers, she suggests they do three things. First, each member of the design team creates his or her own rough draft of the One-Pager. Second, each member of the group shares his or her draft, and the group improves the document by bringing together the most useful information from each draft. Third, the team further refines the document by sharing it with someone who does not know about the document to get feedback about what is clear or unclear. The feedback from readers ultimately increases clarity. Just the art of explaining to someone else who is not "in the know" adds greatly to refining for clarity.

» Each team member writes a rough draft of the One-Pager.
» Collectively the group refines the document using information from the individual drafts.
» The team shares the One-Pager with people who are not familiar with the strategy, and then refines the One-Pager based on their feedback.

Since the process of creating the components of a playbook is fundamentally one of editing, we will now describe the editing process for each of the five elements recommended for the One-Pager with an emphasis on how to keep the teacher perspective in mind.

IN ONE SENTENCE

The first section of the One-Pager is a single sentence stating what the strategy is and what it does. This brief summary makes it easier for teachers to decide whether to implement the strategy to hit their goal. Keeping the statement to one sentence forces the people developing the strategy to know the strategy well enough to describe it succinctly.

To create it, the authors should answer the question, "What is this strategy, and what does it do?" in as many sentences as they wish. After they have written a complete answer to the question, the authors edit the statement and pare it down to one clear sentence that clearly explains the strategy. The mere process of editing the initial descriptions gives participants a deeper understanding of the practice before diving into the research.

THE RESEARCH

In the playbook workshops Ann facilitates, she finds that many coaches see the research section as the most challenging. However, after they understand the research and have written a research section, coaches report that they feel more confident explaining to teachers the advantages of particular strategies.

Dr. Karen Norris, who oversees the education of children in mental health care settings, found that writing the research section helped her team better understand which teaching strategies belong in the playbook. "My biggest learning moments were, first of all, playing with the Hattie Check (Jim's term for the research section of the One-Pager in *The Impact Cycle* [Knight, 2017]). It made me really think about the practices that we had in place and their effectiveness. A specific practice might not have a large effect size, but what's its leverage for us with a school that focuses on social-emotional health? It lends such clarity to our work."

With all of the research available, the playbook design team must step into the teachers' shoes and ask of each study, "Does this research indicate that this is one of the best options for these goals for our student population?" Once team members have analyzed as many studies as possible in this way, they can reduce the answers to a bullet list of key research findings.

THE PURPOSE

The third section of the One-Pager, the purpose statement, summarizes the types of changes teachers should see in their students and how and why that change occurs when using a given strategy. Articulating that purpose clearly and succinctly comes after a thorough examination of the strategy and what it looks like in classroom practice. As Joel Beyenhoff explained when we asked him about his experiences creating the playbook, "I think when we understand a strategy's purpose at a deeper level, it makes it easier to select because, for example, not every strategy that supports student collaboration is a fit for every classroom, or every coaching cycle, or for every goal that a teacher has." A clear purpose statement helps teachers connect the strategy with students' goals. When that connection is not clear, teachers should take the strategy off the list of options.

The authors of the playbook should also examine the strategy for its fit with school or system instructional frameworks to ensure that school and system leaders can support teachers' use of it. Indeed, it is important that school leaders receive professional development so that they have a sufficiently deep understanding of each strategy in the playbook. As Hilary Herrmann, professional learning coordinator, Poudre School District, Fort Collins, Colorado, told us during our interview of her, "Even if it does align with the goals of the system, does everybody understand how it supports those [goals]?"

Once again, after examining all of the evidence about a teaching strategy, the authors should write down all of the information they may want to include in the purpose category. Then they should edit that material down to a short but comprehensive list that explains exactly what the strategy does and how it works.

HOW TEACHERS USE IT

Over the years, we have heard many researchers and leaders comment on teachers' poor implementation of teaching strategies.

We believe that when teacher implementation lacks fidelity to a model, it tends to be a professional development problem rather than a teacher problem. The lack of fidelity to new practices shows up when there is a lack of clarity about how a strategy should be taught, and as Heath and Heath (2010) wrote, "sometimes resistance is just lack of clarity" (p. 15).

The One-Pager summarizes what teachers do to plan, prepare, teach, and evaluate a strategy with students. When the playbook design team creates a powerful, concise, and easy-to-understand document, teachers implementing strategies have a greater chance of being successful, especially when supported by instructional coaches.

HOW STUDENTS USE IT

Sometimes during professional development and coaching, we overlook an important question: "What are the students doing when they use this strategy?" For this section of the One-Pager, the coach lists every action that students take when using the strategy. This kind of clarity helps teachers determine if their students need the strategy and if changes need to be made to the strategy so that it can better respond to students' needs.

For this part of the One-Pager, coaches again write down everything they can glean about student actions from the research and strategy materials and then edit that list so that it fits onto the single page with the other four elements. Even though student use may not apply to all strategies (e.g., for some lesson planning strategies), we suggest that teams at least consider it as they create the One-Pager. After all, everything we are doing is being done to improve students' learning and well-being.

POSSIBLE EXTENSIONS—AND A CAUTION

Our catchphrase throughout much of this book has been to keep the playbook "lean and clean." The shorter, the simpler, the more precise the playbook is, the more useful it will be for teachers.

Nevertheless, we would like to mention two elements that could be added to the One-Pager: data and video. However, the One-Pager, as its name suggests, must remain one page, so if the following additions make the One-Pager too complicated, skip them.

One possible extension to the playbook is a section on data collection tools. This section can describe how data could be collected when a given strategy is used and whether data involve student work, observation, student feedback, or some combination of those data pieces. Data collection forms could also be linked to those lists if the playbook is housed online.

Another possible addition is video. Joi Lunsford's playbook is housed in a Google Folder, so she is able to link videos of teachers and students using specific strategies in the classroom so that teachers have that real-life snapshot of the strategy in action. April Strong, an Instructional Coach in the Martin County School District in Stuart, Florida, likes the idea of linking videos to the One-Pagers, too. She hears teachers use the phrase, "What does it look like?" all the time. She finds that video helps to bring new practices to a "digestible level" for teachers in a coaching practice that she hopes will be the "ripple that causes a tsunami of change" for teachers and students.

When deciding on the content of the One-Pager, keep it simple and always keep teachers and students' perspectives at the fore. The playbook should show different options for student improvement in the simplest terms possible. Dr. Karen Norris compares it to a road map: "Say I want to go from Texas to California, California being the goal. There are multiple routes to get to California, but what are the efficient routes? What are the most effective ways? I think the playbook outlines that." Showing the teacher various effective routes to the goal in the simplest language helps both the coach and the teacher to understand the practices more deeply and more clearly.

MAKING IT REAL

When a team comes together and creates a playbook, leaders might be tempted to take a top-down approach to implementation, telling teachers they must teach the strategies and then creating accountability measures to ensure teachers are kept "accountable," which is a nice way of saying "ensuring that teachers are doing what they are told."

We feel that a top-down implementation model is problematic for at least three reasons. First, telling someone what to do communicates the message that we don't believe they can learn for themselves. Professional development should be empowering, helping people to learn for themselves. However, telling people what to do is disempowering and creates dependence, a school filled who teachers who utter the disheartening phrase, "Just tell me what to do, and I'll do it."

Second, as found and communicated throughout our two decades of research and writing, telling people what to do is a poor strategy. Educators are, to use Peter Drucker's (1969) phrase, "knowledge workers," and they want to think for themselves. Additionally, people are less likely to embrace something that they have no choice about. A top-down model might get begrudging compliance, but it won't lead to high levels of motivation and commitment.

Third, the focus for professional development and professional learning should be on students, not on strategies. For teachers to implement and master teaching strategies, those strategies have to be contextualized to each individual teacher's classroom, which is a fancy way of saying they have to be adapted until they make a difference for children. When a coach helps teachers adapt strategies to the unique needs of students, then strategies start to make a difference.

TO SUM UP

The One-Pager is a single-page description of a strategy that helps a teacher to choose a strategy for a PEERS goal. It aids in communication between the coach and the teacher by condensing the vast amount of information on a strategy into a simple and easy-to-understand summary that conveys the power of the strategy in the classroom.

Understanding the research that supports strategies allows the coach to choose the best strategies for the playbook and to convey the power of the strategies to teachers more clearly and effectively.

The One-Pager consists of five parts: (a) a one-sentence description of the strategy, (b) a description of the research supporting its use, (c) a summary of the strategy's purpose, (d) a description of how teachers use it, and (e) a description of how students use it.

REFLECTION QUESTIONS

1. What was most valuable about this chapter?

2. Do you think your team should create One-Pagers?

3. When creating One-Pagers, how might you navigate the task of approaching the research section for those stategies?

4. Which additional resources do you still need to create One-Pagers?

There are many great books on how effective teams work together, but a few stand out to us. First, a classic work on the topic of teams is Patrick Lencioni's *Five Dysfunctions of a Team: A Leadership Fable* (2002), which we prefer in the manga version. Lencioni tells the story of Kathyrn Petersen and the five dysfunctions:

1. Absence of trust
2. Fear of conflict
3. Lack of commitment
4. Avoidance of accountability
5. Inattention to results

In that book, Ms. Petersen's actions provide a map of how to create a healthy team.

Another useful book on the topic of teams is Judith Glaser's *Conversational Intelligence: How Great Leaders Build Trust and Get Extraordinary Results* (2016). Glaser translates the research on neuroscience into practical communication strategies we can use to move from positional conversations to co-constructed conversations. She emphasizes the importance of trust, integrity, empathy, and good judgment as guiding principles for conversations and shares many important conversational tools and rituals.

Additionally, we have been following Amy Edmondson's research for a long time. Her recent book, *The Fearless Organization: Creating Psychological Safety in the Workplace for Learning, Innovation, and Growth* (2019), is likely her best and most useful. Edmondson believes that learning is vital to any organization, and that learning is impossible without psychological safety (a concept she has been studying for 20 years). In this book, she describes why fearless organizations are essential and how to create ones that flourish because people embrace the opportunity to learn from each other.

Finally, people who want to feel more confident about reading educational research may wish to read Patricia Lauer's *An Education Research Primer: How to Understand, Evaluate, and Use It* (2005).

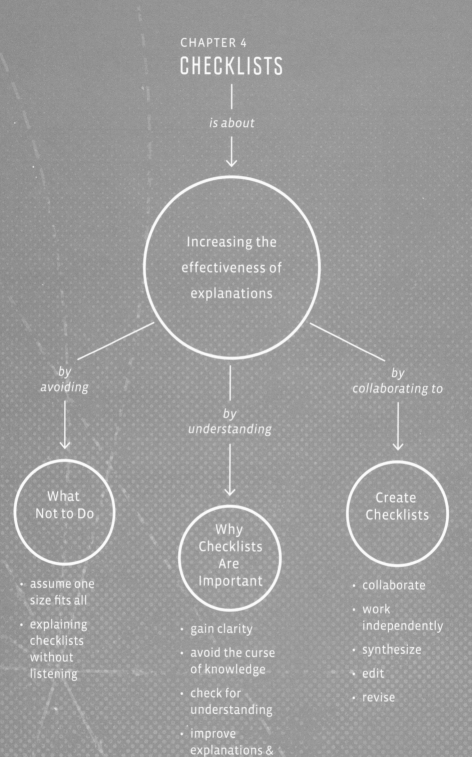

CHAPTER 4
CHECKLISTS

is about

Increasing the effectiveness of explanations

by avoiding

by understanding

by collaborating to

What Not to Do

- assume one size fits all
- explaining checklists without listening

Why Checklists Are Important

- gain clarity
- avoid the curse of knowledge
- check for understanding
- improve explanations & implementation

Create Checklists

- collaborate
- work independently
- synthesize
- edit
- revise

04

CHECKLISTS

 SNAPSHOT:

This chapter goes into detail about what to do and not do when using and sharing checklists, why they are important, and how to create them. If you plan to create and share checklists, we recommend that you read the chapter.

We need a different strategy for overcoming failure, one that builds on experience and takes advantage of the knowledge people have but somehow also makes up for our inevitable human inadequacies. And there is such a strategy, though it will seem almost ridiculous in its simplicity, maybe even crazy to those of us who have spent years carefully developing ever more advanced skills and technologies. It is a checklist.

ATUL GAWANDE

The Checklist Manifesto: How to Get Things Right

In 2015 Sage Publishing celebrated its 50th anniversary, and Jim was fortunate to attend the party. The event was special for two reasons. Most important, the good work that has been done by Sage to promote social science research, guided by founder Sara Miller McCune, deserved to be celebrated. In truth, though, Jim was excited to be there for a second reason. The featured speaker at the evening get-together was none other than Alan Alda, who has written about and studied communication for decades but is better known as the star of the mega-hit TV show M*A*S*H. As a big M*A*S*H fan, Jim was excited to hear what Mr. Alda had to say about communication, but he was also more than a little excited just to be in the same room as Hawkeye Pierce.

As part of his talk about communication, Alda did a fascinating demonstration. He invited a smart young Sage employee to the front of the room as a volunteer and went on to show her a list of three songs, songs that everyone in the room would know such as "God Bless America," "Happy Birthday," and "You Are My Sunshine." Then he explained that she was going to tap out the melody of the songs (by tapping a coin against the podium) and ask the audience to name the song.

Before she starting tapping, Alda asked her, "How many people do you think will recognize the songs?" Without any hesitation, the volunteer said, "Oh, at least 90%." Then she tapped the first song, and when Alda asked the audience to name the song, no one got it right. The same happened for the two other songs.

After thanking his volunteer, Alda explained that the same thing happens to every volunteer. The problem is, he explained, the "curse of knowledge." When we know something extremely well, we assume others will pick it up right away. In reality, our level of knowledge actually makes it more difficult for us to communicate.

In *Made to Stick: Why Some Ideas Survive and Others Die* (2007), Heath and Heath describe the curse of knowledge, a term originally coined by Camerer, Loewenstein, and Weber (1989). According to the authors, our knowledge can interfere with our ability to communicate affectively: "Once we know something, we find it hard to imagine what it was like not to know it. Our knowledge has cursed us. And it becomes difficult for us to share our knowledge with others because we can't readily re-create our listeners' state of mind" (p. 20).

One way to combat the curse of knowledge is to use checklists. When Jim came to the University of Kansas Center for Research on Learning (KUCRL) and began studying professional development with his colleagues, one of the first discoveries he and his colleagues made was that checklists are helpful, if not essential, tools for communicating about teaching strategies. They recognized that if they wanted teachers to implement practices effectively, they needed to describe those practices precisely. After all, people cannot teach what they don't know, and checklists help us explain strategies better, which means teachers understand them better.

Given this interest in checklists, the researchers at what eventually became the Kansas Coaching Project at KUCRL were fascinated when Atul Gawande published his *New Yorker* article describing his research on checklists, which he later expanded into a *New York Times* bestseller and one of our favorite books, *The Checklist Manifesto: How to Get Things Right* (2009). As he explains in his TED talk, "How Do We Heal Medicine?," Gawande was as surprised as anyone that he would be studying checklists. "I did not expect to be spending a significant part of my time as a Harvard surgeon worrying about checklists. And yet what we found [was] that these were tools to help make experts better."

In partnership with the World Health Organization, Gawande conducted a study to assess the impact of a surgical checklist in eight hospitals around the world, deliberately choosing a wide range of settings, with four hospitals from wealthier countries (United States, Canada, New Zealand, and England) and four from poorer countries (Tanzania, Jordon, India, and the Philippines). The results were stunning: When checklists were used by surgical teams, the complication rates in all hospitals fell by an average of 35%, and death rates fell by 47%. Largely as a result of this research, checklists have been adopted widely in hospitals as an essential part of effective medical care. If you have visited a hospital recently, you have probably seen someone using a checklist.

Since the publication of *The Checklist Manifesto*, many educational leaders have been excited about the power of checklists to gain clarity, but as is often the case when something becomes very popular, a small backlash has risen up against the widespread use of checklists. Some argue that the art of teaching cannot be reduced to a simplistic 15-item checklist, or that telling teachers to use a checklist exactly as it is written de-professionalizes teaching and ignores teacher expertise.

We agree with these criticisms. Used incorrectly, checklists can inhibit learning. However, used correctly, checklists are vitally important power tools for learning. Therefore, before discussing how to use checklists to increase the impact of professional development, we will discuss three common mistakes and how to avoid them: (a) Assuming a simplistic list captures all that is important for the complex art of teaching; (b) assuming that one size fits all; and (c) explaining checklists without listening.

Three Mistakes to Avoid When Using Checklists

1. Assuming a simplistic list captures all that is important for the complex art of teaching

If you are a parent, you know how challenging it can be to raise a child. All children experience unique developmental and social-emotional issues, including such concerns as self-doubt, being accepted by others, being treated fairly, feeling safe, and many, many other issues. And if you parent two or more children, you learn pretty quickly that each child is an individually wired unique bundle of potential, joy, and challenge. As a result, what works for one child doesn't necessarily work for another.

To demonstrate how complex teaching is, let's compare it to parenting 25 or more children. One student in the classroom may misunderstand a foundational concept and be confused by a lesson. Another may be totally focused on what a friend just said about him during break. Some students face other, sometimes heart-breaking issues. They might be hungry. They might be tired. They might be afraid of being bullied or suffering other forms of abuse.

Teaching is one of the most complex professions, and that is why we believe that trying to create a simplistic checklist for teaching will do more harm than good. Teachers must adapt to each student as best as they can. Each class is its own unique learning culture: What works at 8:15 might not work at 2:15, and what works with one student might not work with another; in fact, the same thing might not work with the same student later in the same day.

Given such complexity, any attempt to create a simple checklist for all of teaching is likely doomed to fail. Checklists dramatically increase the precision and clarity of our explanations of particular teaching strategies and practices within strategies. Checklists can be used for at least four purposes: (a) to describe how to do something, such as write guiding questions for a unit; (b) to describe quality characteristics, such as the characteristics of effective learning maps; (c) to describe what teachers do; and (d) to describe what students do. However, the broad sweep of all that is good and beautiful in teaching cannot and should not be summarized in a dumbed-down checklist. The complexity of the art and science of teaching goes far beyond any simple itemized checklist.

CHECKLISTS DESCRIBE

» How to do something

» What a quality product looks like

» What teachers do

» What students do

2. Assuming that one size fits all

In some school districts, coaches are expected to ensure that teachers implement the teaching strategies from the playbook with fidelity. Such a focus on fidelity grows out of good intentions: Leaders want teachers to use strategies in the way that research indicates works best, and certainly coaches need to support teachers in achieving high-quality implementation of teaching strategies. However, it is results that matter—significant positive improvements in student learning and well-being. After more than two decades studying coaching, we have concluded that too narrow a focus on fidelity can inhibit learning. There are at least three reasons why this is true.

First, a strict focus on fidelity sends a message to teachers that leaders view reform in this manner: "We identified the problem, we picked the solution to the problem, and now we want you to implement the solution we chose for you and do it exactly as we tell you to do it." The parental tone of that message discounts teachers' knowledge, experience, capacity, and especially their knowledge of their individual students, and it encourages teacher resistance in taking on the new strategy.

Second, telling teachers to implement exactly the steps of a checklist often decreases teacher motivation. An overemphasis on fidelity may lead to teachers doing every move on a checklist but without passion, or love, and even in ways that fail to promote reflection. As Thomas Davenport has shown in *Thinking for a Living: How to Get Better Performances and Results from Knowledge Workers* (2005), when professionals such as teachers are not given the opportunity to reflect and think for themselves, they resist change. Simply put: What knowledge workers, in this case teachers, do is think for a living; if someone else (researchers, administrators, policy makers) does the thinking for teachers, teachers will resist.

Third, the notion that an educational practice works the same way in every district, school, and classroom and for every individual student is great in theory, but students are complex human beings who require different approaches depending on where they are in their life and learning. Teachers, too, have different strengths, so most teaching strategies will look different in different hands. We are fond of quoting Eric Lui (2006), who has insightfully written that "in education, it's never one size fits all—it's one size fits one" (p. 47).

We all want the best possible instruction for students. Checklists help because they increase the precision of conversations about teaching practices. Goals also increase the effectiveness of instruction by providing an objective standard of excellence that teachers own, as opposed to a standard imposed on them. Finally, listening to teachers and taking a dialogical approach increases teacher commitment to and ownership of strategies. Our guess is that listening to teachers leads to higher fidelity to teaching practices because, when teachers have a voice in their learning, they will be more committed to whatever strategy they are implementing.

Breaking away from a narrow focus on fidelity to encouraging more teacher choice and dialogue can be challenging, but Iowa principal Joel Beyerof believes it is crucial. He compares the issue of fidelity versus partnership to baking versus cooking:

> In baking, you just follow a recipe and then just leave it alone. That's very teacher centered: there are specific moves; you don't change; it's all exactly the same every time. In cooking, you have refinement: you sample what you use and make adjustments. That's formative assessment, and we're constantly tweaking. Even though the playbook might have a selection of strategies to choose from, the checklist is going to be personalized to that group of teachers or individual teacher using it based on their student needs.

3. Explaining checklists without listening

Conversations about checklists should not be one way, with the coach telling the teacher what to do without asking for feedback from the teacher, expecting the teacher to do just what they are told. Teachers have a lot of knowledge about students and about teaching, and that knowledge must be valued, not just because that's the respectful way to interact, but because that knowledge is important.

What is more, telling and not listening is not an effective communication strategy. As Stephen Covey (1989) points out, "If you want to interact effectively with me, to influence me—your spouse, your child, your neighbor, your boss, your co-worker, your friend —you first need to understand me" (p. 238). We see checklists as a point of departure for dialogue, not a list of non-negotiables to be carried out the same way every time.

What we have learned through our partnerships with coaches and other educators is that, after coaches have done the deep work of creating checklists for an instructional playbook, they should share the ready-made checklists with teachers precisely but provisionally. When coaches are precise, they explain each item on the checklist clearly and in a such a way that makes it easy for a collaborating teacher to understand how to implement what is being described. Checklists contain what Chris Argyris (2005) refers to as "actionable knowledge," and good explanations clearly state how teachers are to act if they implement an item on the checklist.

When coaches are provisional with their explanations, they share the items on a checklist tentatively, checking with the teacher after each item is explained to see if that is the way the teacher wants to implement the strategy and also whether or not the teacher wants to add something to the checklist. Often, because of their knowledge of their students and their ability as professionals, teachers suggest revisions that improve the teaching plan embodied in the checklist.

However, if a teacher wants to make a modification that the coach considers ill advised, the coach should share her or his thoughts in a tentative way, while still positioning the teacher as the decision maker. For example, a coach might say, "Do you mind if I share a concern?" If the teacher invites the coach to share, the coach can say something like, "Well, you know your students best and what is best for them, so I may be all wrong here, but my concern is if you don't allow students to practice before they work independently, they may struggle with the task, and then you'll have to teach it all over again. What do you think?"

In some cases, the teacher will agree with the coach and change her plans. In other cases, the teacher will stick with her plan and say something like, "I think I'll stick with my plan and see what happens." The coach can then say, "Let's try it out. We've got a goal. Let's see if we hit the goal. If not, we can come back to the checklist and try it again."

Two things are important here. First, we have found that the initial implementation of any strategy usually does not work well without some adaptation. Second, coaches need to take a humble approach, acknowledging the complexity of the classroom. Each student is such a unique individual that no strategy can be guaranteed to succeed.

We don't like checklists. They can be painstaking. They're not much fun. But I don't think the issue here is mere laziness. There's something deeper, more visceral going on when people walk away not only from saving lives but from making money. It somehow feels beneath us to use a checklist, an embarrassment. It runs counter to deeply held beliefs about how the truly great among us—those we aspire to be—handle situations of high stakes and complexity. The truly great are daring. They improvise. They do not have protocols and checklists. Maybe our idea of heroism needs updating.

ATUL GAWANDE

The Checklist Manifesto: How to Get Things Right (p.173)

The Necessity of Checklists

As soon as our research team started studying how video recordings could support coaching, we found that every coach we partnered with said basically the same thing: "I don't know how I coached before I started to use video." Almost the same comment was made by us and everyone else we worked with when we saw the value of using checklists. The lowly checklist, as we explain below, is a power tool for professional learning.

CHECKLISTS AND THE ART AND SCIENCE OF TEACHING

Teaching is often described as both an art and a science. In fact, Merriam-Webster's Dictionary defines pedagogy as "the art, science, or profession of teaching." The science of teaching gives us processes and procedures to follow (lesson plans, attendance rosters, bell schedules, etc.). But the artistry of teaching? Art is something altogether different.

Internationally recognized marketing and leadership expert Seth Godin has written lyrically about each person's need to be an artist. In *The Icarus Deception: How High Will You Fly?* (2012), Godin argues that we only fully realize our humanity when we strike out to be artists. "A revolution is here," Godin writes, "and it is shining a light on what we've known deep down for a long time—you are capable of making a difference, of being bold, and of changing more than you are willing to admit. You are capable of making art" (p. 2).

"Art is not a gene or a specific talent. Art is an attitude, culturally driven and available to anyone who chooses to adopt it. Art isn't something sold in a gallery or performed on a stage. Art is the unique work of a human being, work that touches another .... Seizing new ground, making connections between people or ideas, working without a map—these are works of art, and if you do them, you are an artist, regardless of whether you wear a smock, use a computer, or work with others all day long. Speaking up when there's no obvious right answer, making yourself vulnerable when it's possible to put up shields, and caring about both the process and the outcome—these are works of art that our society embraces and the economy demands" (pp. 6-7).

To truly support teachers, coaches need to straddle both worlds, art and science. Explaining the required components of a lesson plan to new teachers is easy (science), but explaining how to make a particular lesson plan responsive to individual student needs is not (art). Similarly, explaining the steps of a cooperative learning activity is easy (science), but explaining how specific students' academic, behavioral, and interpersonal skills should influence how the teacher most effectively groups students for a specific outcome is not (art). Coaches must navigate this challenging territory by recognizing that teaching involves two kinds of knowledge: tacit and explicit.

TACIT KNOWLEDGE VS. EXPLICIT KNOWLEDGE

Tacit knowledge was first described by polymath Michael Polanyi (1966), whose ideas shaped economics, chemistry, philosophy, and our understanding of science. Polanyi's ideas were integrated into a theory of organizational learning in a fascinating study of Japanese businesses written by Ikujir Nonaka and Hirotaka Takeuchi, *The Knowledge Creating Company: How Japanese Companies Create the Dynamics of Innovation* (1995).

Tacit knowledge, as Nonaka and Takeuchi (1995) explained, "is hard to articulate with formal language. It is personal knowledge embedded in individual experience and involves intangible factors such as personal belief, perspective, and the value system" (p. viii). As the authors explain, "Polanyi contends that human beings acquire knowledge by actively creating and organizing their own experiences. Thus, knowledge that can be expressed in words and numbers represents only the tip of the iceberg of the entire body of knowledge" (p. viii).

There is a tacit dimension to the work done by any skillful practitioner, including teachers. Polanyi says, "we can know more than we can tell" (Nonanka & Takeuchi, 1995, p. 4), and that is certainly true of excellent teachers. There is the information in manuals and research articles, and then there are the artistic elements that outstanding teachers may not even realize they know or do. The art of teaching may involve a tone of voice, facial expressions, ways of moving about the classroom, and any number of approaches to encouraging students that great teachers do without even knowing they do them.

The challenge is that if we don't know we're doing something, we can't describe what we're doing, and if we have can't describe something, we can't share it with someone else. That is why the second form of knowledge is important. Explicit knowledge can be described, stated, written in manuals, and, as is most relevant here, included in checklists. Knowledge transfer involves making tacit knowledge explicit, and then helping others internalize that knowledge. Instructional coaches do this by being precise and provisional with their explanations, and then by partnering with teachers to make adaptations to how strategies are implemented until identified goals are met.

THE CURSE OF KNOWLEDGE

As the Alan Alda story at the start of this chapter illustrates, ironically, we sometimes struggle to explain things because we know too much about a topic. The distinction between tacit and explicit knowledge helps explain why too much knowledge can get in the way. When we master something like a teaching strategy, we are often able to implement aspects of it without much conscious thought; that is, we develop tacit knowledge about what we do— knowledge we have but don't realize we have.

Checklists remind us of the steps of a process—they make and keep the tacit knowledge explicit. Using a checklist to explain a strategy ensures that we don't overlook something that we have learned so well that we might forget to explain it. Additionally, checklists slow down our explanations to a pace that our collaborating teacher can manage, which further improves our effectiveness as communicators.

THE "CURSE OF FORGETFULNESS"

We made up this term, but that doesn't make the phenomenon it describes any less real. Checklists are helpful because they ensure that we don't forget crucial aspects of the teaching strategies we describe. Indeed, when Jim published *Instructional Coaching: A Partnership Approach to Improving Knowledge* (Knight, 2007), he suggested that coaches and teachers co-construct checklists so that teachers' voices are active partners in the discussion of how strategies are implemented. As coaches acted on that advice, they realized that they kept forgetting important parts of the strategy. Explaining a strategy in a way that genuinely invites a collaborating teacher's opinion is a complex communication task in and of itself, and when a coach's mental bandwidth is focused on interactive explanation, aspects of a strategy can easily be forgotten during the conversation.

One of the benefits of using a checklist is that it helps us with the curse of forgetfulness and increases our confidence. Hilary Herrmann in Fort Colins, Colorado, describes that feeling of competence: "Because of the pace at which we work, we feel like we know what we are talking about, but then we have these moments of thinking, 'I think I know what that is, but do I really know what that is?' When you have something like checklists and are able to double-check, you can say, 'Yeah, I do know this. I got this. Let's go.'"

FALSE CLARITY

Jim first learned about the concept of false clarity from Michael Fullan when he studied with him at the University of Toronto. According to Fullan (2001), "false clarity occurs when change is interpreted in an oversimplified way; that is, the proposed change has more to it than people perceive or realize" (p. 77).

False clarity, then, is kind of the opposite of the curse of knowledge. That is, with the curse of knowledge, we struggle to provide clear explanations because we know so much that it interferes with our ability to communicate. With false clarity, on the other hand, the problem is that we know less than we actually think we do. We are confident that we are teaching a strategy effectively, but in reality we're doing it in ways that are completely different from what researchers suggest.

False clarity is everywhere, and it is easy to understand why. Books or articles describing teaching practices can be very complex to understand, and it can be difficult to remember everything we have read, no matter how carefully we study. Then in the classroom, we unintentionally leave out aspects of a practice. Over time, we develop a habitual way of teaching a strategy that is quite a bit different from what research says about how to teach it.

As we have emphasized throughout this book, teaching strategies need to be adapted to better meet the unique needs of classrooms filled with uniquely different children. However, adaptations should be by design, not by omission. If we are going to change a practice, we first need to know what it is that we are changing, and that is not possible if a coach has false clarity.

"If I don't know I don't know, I think I know."
//////////////

R. D. LAING
Knots

Kristina Feldner, a professional developer in Irving Independent School District in Texas, shared with Ann that she first heard about checklists and the playbook when she attended Ann's session at our annual Teaching Learning Coaching Conference. As a former coach, Kristina and her district were focusing on clarity and consistency around the work of coaches. In talking with coaches, she saw the playbook as a way to bring all of their voices together, an opportunity for everyone on the team to have ownership. She said,

"We didn't have anything like this." She also sees the playbook as increasing the culture of coaching in the district. She said that, while the playbook was a huge undertaking, it was worth every minute: "There is so much value in the process. You can't discount that."

COGNITIVE OVERLOAD

Checklists also help to reduce the cognitive overload teachers may experience if they are given too much information. Amber Thienel in Franklin, Tennessee, told us that this is one of the reasons why she wanted her team to create a playbook. "The biggest challenge so far is that we all had so many ideas about what we thought were best instructional practices. They were all really good, but we knew they had to be simplified or teachers would feel overwhelmed."

Too many strategies overwhelm, and so does too much explanation. Keeping the checklist simple while ensuring that it includes every essential element is captured requires an ongoing balancing act to make implementation more visible and easier for teachers.

CHECKLISTS AS FORMATIVE ASSESSMENT

When coaches share checklists in a precise but provisional way, the checklist also functions as a kind of formative assessment. That is, after coaches explain each item (or a few items) on the checklist, they should pause and ask teachers if they have any questions about the item and whether they want to teach the strategy as it is being explained. That is, after each item is explained, the coach asks the teacher to make a choice, and in order to make a choice ("Will or won't I teach it this way?"), the teacher needs to understand the item. In this way, the simple act of giving teachers control over what they teach also increases understanding. Each time the coach stops and checks with the teacher, the coach is conducting a kind of formative assessment.

Stopping and checking is a way of allowing each teacher's internal conversation to become external because whenever a coach is explaining a teaching strategy, the listening teacher is asking the same two questions: "Do I understand this?" "Do I want to teach it this way or change it?"

CHECKLISTS AS POWER TOOLS

At the most basic level, checklists serve many purposes in addition to everything else listed here. Teachers can use the checklist to remind themselves of the essential elements of a strategy before they implement it for the first few times. Additionally, they can use checklists to help them focus their attention on essential elements of a teaching strategy when they watch video recordings of their lesson or when they watch coaches or others implement the strategy. Also, when requested by teachers, coaches can use checklists to observe and gather data on how teachers implement strategies. This is not as powerful as when teachers watch their own video of their lessons, but it can save teachers a significant amount of time if coach and teacher have a truly trusting relationship.

Checklists also enhance communication between teachers and coaches and between coaches and administrators. The process of creating checklists and uncovering each team member's tacit knowledge of a teaching practice gives everyone involved a greater understanding of the practice and the complexities of its implementation.

Finally, using checklists with teachers can not only expand the ways in which both coach and teacher think about a specific practice but also reinforce elements of best practices beyond the scope of a specific goal. Michelle Kavars, a strategist who works with the teachers of gifted students in Lewis Central School in Iowa, describes the growth she has seen in how teachers approach the learning of their gifted students as a result of using a checklist.

One of the checklists that I use most often is the one that's been refined the most: the one on offering choices. There are a couple of questions at the beginning of that checklist that I think have really changed some teacher thinking. We always start with the standard or the learning question, and that reinforces that gifted kids should be a part of our instruction, and our instruction starts with a standards-based desire for them to learn. That applies to all kids. I ask teachers who their audience is for offering choices.

With gifted and advanced learners, there's still a preconceived notion in the back of teachers' minds that gifted kids could be given a packet and work off to the side by themselves. That's not ideal, that's not best practice, and that's not part of our instructional practice, so when we talk through that question of who is their audience, teachers can be thinking about, "Am I doing this in response to pre-assessment data? Am I doing this in response to student work? Have I looked at some student writing and some exit tickets and realize that I have kids who could be working at a greater level of challenge?" I think teachers are becoming more flexible in how they think about the learners in their classroom, but I also like that [gifted education is] not this random thing that is occurring off to the side. It is part of what we do, and we should be held to the same high-quality standards for our gifted kids as we are for the rest of the student population.

CHECKLISTS AS A THIRD POINT FOR DIALOGUE

Much has been written about the importance of a third point, or what Parker Palmer (2009) calls "third things," for dialogue. According to Palmer, we can promote dialogue and meaningful conversation by using "third things" to turn the focus of the conversation away from the people in the conversation and toward something external.

This "thing" could be a poem, story, piece of music, or a work that embodies [the topic for discussion]. Palmer writes:

> I call these embodiments "third things" because they represent neither the voice of the facilitator nor the voice of the participant...Mediated by a third thing, truth can emerge from, and return to, our awareness at whatever pace and depth we are able to handle— sometimes inwardly in silence, sometimes aloud in community—giving the shy soul the protective cover it needs. (pp. 92-93)

The idea is that when two or more people have a "third thing" to discuss (a video clip of a lesson, student work, an article, a checklist), the focus turns away from the individuals and toward that thing, which is to say, the conversation becomes more back-and-forth or dialogical. As Paulo Freire explained in much of his writing, dialogue melts away the coach's role as coach and the teacher's role as teacher, and both people in the interaction become learners and teachers, teaching and learning with each other.

The same thing can occur when coaches effectively share checklists with teachers. The coach does explain the strategy, but as the coach explains the strategy, teacher and coach equally and dialogically explore how the strategy might need to be adapted to best meet the needs of students.

This kind of back-and-forth dialogical conversation is crucial because teachers have a wealth of knowledge in one area that is beyond the scope of the people who created, or the coach who explains, a checklist. Teachers have a deeper knowledge of their needs as teachers as well as the specific needs of their students. Asking directly for teacher voice when explaining the checklist can not only increase partnership and enhance the coaching relationship; it also can improve implementation.

In Jim's video series with Crysta Crum, accompanying *The Impact Cycle: What Instructional Coaches Should Do to Foster Powerful Improvements in Teaching* (2017), one can see that Jim directly encourages Crysta to modify the checklist for response cards as she sees fit. Jim may know a great deal about formative assessment, but he has never taught fourth graders. Crysta is the expert on her fourth graders, and she knows that they will require a certain level of practice with specific elements of the strategy to implement it well. Jim's and Crysta's conversation is a dialogue, one where each person's expertise plays an important role in creating the best learning environments for students.

Dr. Karen Norris in Texas values dialogue with teachers about the checklists, not only as part of The Impact Cycle but also as part of refining the playbook. "The checklists were a way for us to have a common language about practices. Our team would outline a checklist in a certain way, and then teachers would see it and say, 'Oh my gosh, I haven't been doing that.' We could all revisit it and say, 'OK, is this what we really want?'" Discussing those practices and their checklists together only enhanced the level of communication about teaching in their schools, so much so that Dr. Norris emphasizes, "I cannot say enough that having such clarity across administrative and teacher staff is really huge."

Creating Checklists

Because each strategy potentially involves multiple Checklists, creating the Checklists for a playbook may appear to be time-consuming, but participants in our playbook workshops report that the opposite is true. By the time the playbook team has created the Table of Contents and the One-Pagers, the team has typically established norms, processes, and perhaps even a "rhythm" of working together that makes the process more efficient than one might expect.

COLLABORATE

As with the other parts of the playbook, the process for creating the Checklists relies on editing, but collaboration is perhaps more crucial during the creation of Checklists than for any other part of the playbook. Michelle once worked with a coach who brought different checklists for the same strategy to her coaching sessions and changed them according to what the teacher shared about her students. For Michelle, it was powerful to listen to the back-and-forth thinking of genuine dialogue. She believes that the coach created the opportunity for dialogue by asking the teacher to choose the checklist she thought was best for her students' goal and her classroom environment. That is, by positioning her collaborating teacher as the decision maker right from the start, the coach made it much easier for teacher and coach to have a conversation where they were thinking together.

CREATE INDEPENDENTLY

The first step in creating a checklist is to have everyone create their own unique checklist without anyone else's assistance to ensure that no important information is overlooked. When everyone creates an individual checklist first, more items will be included, and the team is less likely to leave out important information. If two or more team members co-create a checklist

---

"We always hope for the easy fix: the one simple change that will erase a problem in a stroke. But few things in life work this way. Instead, success requires making a hundred small steps go right - one after the other, no slip ups, no goofs, everyone pitching in."

//////////////

ATUL GAWANDE

Better: A Surgeon's Notes on Performance (2007) (p.21)

without working on their own first, they may influence each other's thinking so much that important pieces of information are overlooked. In short, working individually first leads to a better final product.

SYNTHESIZE

To make it easier to see and learn from everyone else's checklists, we suggest each person writes his or her checklist on chart paper and posts it in the room. Then the group facilitator can ask the group to identify common elements (or specific individual elements that might be grouped into a more general item on a checklist), while writing a common checklist on chart paper or a white board. The facilitator's and team's goal should be to capture all of the critical elements of the teaching practice and (paradoxically) to ensure that the checklist is as concise as possible.

The best checklists have two characteristics: They are comprehensive and concise.

The conversations about checklists are often less contentious and move more quickly than editing down the strategies on the Table of Contents, but there are still potential partnership pitfalls, and team members may need to fight the tendency to become directive with the other members.

When creating checklists with her team, Hilary Hermann found that discussions she had with Jim about the playbook at a conference were helpful in her understanding of the process but made facilitating a team approach to checklists challenging with her colleagues. "After we did the first few, we paused along the way and built some norms around what we want the Checklists to look like. That was a challenge for me in facilitating that work because I had a really clear vision of what I wanted them to look like, and it's hard when everyone in the room has not had access to that learning that I had."

EDIT

When we present the instructional playbook workshop, one slide that always garners a smile is our Checklist for Checklists. Yes, even checklists need a checklist (We couldn't resist!).

To ensure that all of the important elements that make a checklist helpful are included, we suggest that team members scrutinize the checklists they are creating for the following five characteristics in our Checklist for Checklists. This checklist is drawn from the ideas of Daniel Boorman. Boorman, a former pilot, has created many of the checklists developed by Boeing, and he is, therefore, one of the world's leading experts on this topic. He was featured in Gawande's *The Checklist Manifesto*.

CHECKLIST FOR CHECKLISTS

AN EFFECTIVE CHECKLIST IS...	☑
Concise: Less than 10 lines and as short as possible.	○
Explicit: Everything important is stated.	○
Precise: Each item is clearly described.	○
Easy to Understand: Use the right words stated in the simplest way.	○
Comprehensive: Everything that needs to be addressed is addressed.	○

To strip an idea down to its core, we must be masters of exclusion. We must relentlessly prioritize. Saying something short is not the mission—sound bites are not the ideal. Proverbs—a short, profound saying—are the ideal. We must create ideas that are both simple and profound. The Golden Rule is the ultimate model of simplicity: a one-sentence statement so profound that an individual could spend a lifetime learning to follow it.

HEATH & HEATH

Made to Stick: Why Some Ideas Survive and Others Die (2007) (p.16)

MONITOR, IMPROVE, AND REFINE

Among all of the educators we interviewed for this book, a constant refrain was the "living" quality, not only of the playbook itself but of the checklists, in particular. Coaches should have a process in place to examine the modifications that teachers make to strategies during Impact Cycles. Coaches can learn from teachers' individual experiences about changes to the checklist that may be helpful across multiple settings and, therefore, be included for everyone. Coaches can also document modifications that did not help move students closer to the goal for a particular teacher so that other teachers with goals in the same area can benefit from that information as well. The key is having a process in place to examine checklists over and over again for relevance, for modification, and to ensure that they continue to hit each item on the Checklist for Checklists.

Jim included a full instructional playbook at the back of *The Impact Cycle* (Knight, 2017), and readers often tell us that they plan to begin using Jim's playbook as their own to get started using one. This is a fine idea for coaches who prefer to work from that model, but Jim would be the first to encourage coaches to continually examine it, revise it, and reflect on its use.

A colleague of Ellen Dorsey, a math instructional coach with Washington Central Advisory Union 32 in Burlington, Vermont, wanted to use Jim's playbook to start, but Ellen liked the idea of starting from scratch:

> There's a playbook in the back of *The Impact Cycle*, and one of my colleagues said, "Oh, we could just use this." And it's a funny thing, but we are huge on reinventing the wheel here, and I am actually all for reinventing the wheel. By reinventing the wheel, you make it your own, you internalize it, and you bring it into your own context. By using someone else's playbook, you could avoid the messiness of the exercise of creating one, but I like the learning that occurs in the messy space of co-creating something.

Good checklists, on the other hand are precise. They are efficient, to the point, and easy to use even in the most difficult situations. They do not try to spell out everything – a checklist cannot fly a plane. Instead, they provide reminders of only the most critical and important steps – the ones that even the highly skilled professional using them could miss. Good checklists are, above all, practical.

/////////////

ATUL GAWANDE

The Checklist Manifesto: How to Get Things Right (p.120)

Whether you use an existing playbook or create one yourself, the process for improving it should be ongoing. Student needs are ever changing, which means that teacher needs and their goals for their students are ever changing. In the words of Harrison McCoy, instructional content coach, Education Service Center, Region 11, Texas: "A weak playbook would be something that would be a kind of textbook and never evolve." Coaches and teachers should always be learning as they support student learning, and that learning should be documented in the playbook and especially in the playbook's checklists.

Some teachers have a negative response to the term "checklist." It can feel like a mandate. It can feel restrictive and judgmental. Teachers may think, "You can't capture everything a teacher has to do in a lesson in a checklist," and they're right. Teaching is too complex for such limited thinking.

Therefore, the checklists we describe are not mandates, restrictive, or judgmental. They are tools, created in an environment of partnership, to help teachers get better at what they do. In a profession where change is constant and the responsibility is intense, the humble checklist can foster clarity and confidence on improvements as teachers work to create the best learning environments for students.

 ## MAKING IT REAL

To make the checklists real, practice the process for creating them. Gather with a group of colleagues who all have experience with the same teaching strategy. Ask each person to create a checklist for the strategy separately from everyone else. Then come together and compare the checklists. Combine all of the elements in order and then edit them down to make the checklist as concise as possible. Check the draft against the Checklist for Checklists to ensure that each element of an effective checklist is in place. Afterward, reflect on the process and identify any norms you may need to set once you begin work on the playbook or any modifications you may need to make to the process.

Ann has used the following process to help coaches refine their checklists. After creating a checklist, the coach finds someone who is unfamiliar with the teaching practice and shares the checklist with that person just as the coach would with a teacher. This exercise helps to clarify and refine the checklist through the questions that the learner asks about the practice. It can also alert the coach to tacit knowledge issues in the checklist and give the coach practice in explaining the steps. Video- or audiotaping this practice is helpful as well.

TO SUM UP

Checklists are documents that appear after each One-Pager and explain the minimum number of steps necessary to implement instructional strategies.

Checklists require precision in examining both the explicit and tacit knowledge involved in implementing a teaching practice to avoid the problems with clarity caused by the curse of knowledge.

Checklists are provisional and continuously modified because coaches ensure that teachers feel free to adapt every checklist by giving them voice to make modifications through dialogue with the coach regarding student needs.

The process for creating a checklist involves collaboration and a synthesis of individual checklists to create a master draft.

To make checklists effective, the Checklist for Checklists and an ongoing continuous improvement process are critical.

REFLECTION QUESTIONS

1. What was most valuable about this chapter?

2. What reservations if any do you still have about checklists?

3. What other tools and strategies can you use to ensure your explanations are clear and understood?

4. What do you need to do to ensure that your explanations are dialogical rather than directive?

GOING DEEPER

The majority of Atul Gawande's writing circles around one important theme: the best way for professionals to get better at what they do. Although he writes about medicine and surgery, his work is broadly applicable to anyone who wants to improve what they do or works with others who want to improve. We recommend every one of his *New Yorker* articles, but of special interest are "The Checklist," which summarizes his findings about checklists, and "Personal Best," which is about coaching and describes, among other things, Atul's meeting with Jim to observe and discuss coaches. All of Atul's books are similarly helpful to anyone interested in getting better, but for the topic described here, his *The Checklist Manifesto: How to Get Things Right* (2009) is highly engaging, fascinating, and useful.

Chip and Dan Heath's *Made to Stick: Why Some Ideas Survive and Others Die* (2007) is a riff on one of the main ideas in another book, Malcolm Gladwell's *The Tipping Point: How Little Ideas Can Make a Big Difference* (2002), on how to describe ideas in ways that "stick," that remain in our minds. As the authors explain, "if you have to tell someone the same thing ten times, the idea probably wasn't very well designed" (p. 9). The authors assert that memorable ideas are grounded in six principles; simplicity, unexpectedness, concreteness, credibility, emotions, and stories.

Lee Lefever's book *The Art of Explanation: Making Your Ideas, Products, and Services Easier to Understand* (2013) addresses what he refers to as "the explanation problem." "The biggest barrier to adoption," he explains, "is not design, features, or benefits but communication" (p. xx). The book is packed with suggestions for how to communicate ideas with empathy so they connect and clarify what is being explained.

TOOLS FOR CREATING YOUR OWN
INSTRUCTIONAL PLAYBOOK

Resources

Any playbook design team will likely want to refer to a variety of resources. This section is meant to be a starting point for listing books a team might want to look over. By no means complete, this is a list of some of the resources that we have read and found useful or that people we respect have used as they have created their playbooks. To make this list easier to use, we have divided it into four sections:

1. Comprehensive Instructional Books
2. Content Planning
3. Formative Assessment
4. Student Engagement

COMPREHENSIVE INSTRUCTIONAL BOOKS

Many books provide a comprehensive overview of teaching strategies, but the five books below are mentioned by educators around the world as being especially helpful.

HIGH-IMPACT INSTRUCTION

Not surprisingly, Jim's *High-Impact Instruction* (Knight, 2013) provides many tools that help educators create playbooks, including checklists for all of the 16 teaching strategies it describes and video clips of teachers using and discussing those strategies. The book is organized around the framework Jim refers to as The Big Four: Content Planning, Formative Assessment, Instruction, and Community Building. Many teams creating their own playbooks have adopted that framework for their playbooks and incorporated the checklists in their books into their playbooks. We think the book is a go-to resource for anyone creating an instructional playbook.

VISIBLE LEARNING

John Hattie's *Visible Learning: A Synthesis of Over 800 Meta-Analyses Relating to Achievement* (2008) is one of the most influential educational research books of the past few decades. Hattie identifies the most important factors in increasing achievement by synthesizing meta-analyses of research studies and calculating effect sizes for the most common variables related to achievement.

There are many other books related to Visible Learning, including texts focused on literacy (Fisher, Frye, & Hattie, 2016), mathematics (Hattie et al., 2016), and science (Almarode, Fisher, Frey, & Hattie, 2018), and other books exploring Visible Learning more generally. For a broad introduction to Visible Learning, we suggest Hattie and Zierer's *10 Mindframes for Visible Learning: Teaching for Success* (2017), which provides a relatively accessible explanation of the Visible Learning model. Jim's article "Instructional Coaching for Implementing Visible Learning" (2019) is the first paper to study how instructional coaching supports the implementation of Visible Learning.

ART AND SCIENCE OF TEACHING

Similar to Hattie's work, Robert Marzano's *The New Art and Science of Teaching: More Than 50 New Instructional Strategies for Student Success* (2017) identifies effective teaching strategies to increase achievement by reporting on his synthesis of meta-analyses focused on effective size in the education literature. Also, similar to Hattie, many books explore Marzano's research, the most famous of which is Marzano's *Classroom Instruction That Works: Research-Based Strategies for Increasing Student Achievement* (2001). For the purposes of creating an instructional playbook, we have found *The New Art and Science of Teaching* (2107) to be the most helpful.

THE SKILLFUL TEACHER

John Saphier, Mary Ann Haley-Speca, and Robert Gower's *The Skillful Teacher: Building Your Teaching Skills, 6th Edition* (2007) provides a comprehensive overview of teacher beliefs and offers suggestions related to classroom management, including getting students to stay on task, managing the flow of events during a lesson, managing space and time, and suggestions for decreasing disruptions and increasing responsibility. Additionally, the authors include ideas for ensuring that concepts and skills are clearly taught and outline principles for learning and designing effective learning experiences, models of teaching, expectations, relationship building, objectives, and formative assessment. In our experience, there may be no more comprehensive discussion of teaching strategies than this book.

TEACH LIKE A CHAMPION

Doug LeMov's *Teach Like a Champion* (2010) and, more recently, *Teach Like a Champion 2.0* (2015) bring together many teaching strategies that have become a part of the vocabulary on instruction in many schools, including such practices as "No Opt-Out," a strategy for ensuring all students answer questions during class, and "The Hook," a strategy for getting students interested in a lesson by sharing the key and most interesting information about a lesson up front. We especially like the videos that come with the book to illustrate the practices.

CONTENT PLANNING

UNWRAPPING STANDARDS

Larry Ainsworth and Donald Viegut's (2014) work on unwrapping the standards has helped thousands of educators develop a deeper understanding of the standards that are designed to guide their instruction and their students' learning. Ainsworth's big idea is that we should go through standards with care, paying attention to the nouns and verbs, because nouns usually describe knowledge students need to acquire and verbs usually identify skills. He also emphasizes the importance of identifying priority standards since standards such as Common Core list more outcomes than anyone can learn in an academic year. Ainsworth has written many books about what educators can do to better understand standards, but we have found his *Common Formative Assessments 2.0* (2014), written with Donald Viegut, to be especially helpful.

UNDERSTANDING BY DESIGN

Grant Wiggins and Jay McTighe's *Understanding by Design* (2005), also known as UbD,™ has had a big impact on the way educators understand curriculum development. Wiggins and McTighe's concepts of enduring understandings and essential questions have become part of our educational vernacular and will continue to be discussed by educators for years to come. UbD™ provides educators with a process for clarifying learning goals (especially at the unit level), developing formative assessments, and planning lessons.

CONTENT PLANNING: LITERACY

IN THE MIDDLE

Nancy Atwell's *In the Middle: New Understandings About Writing, Reading, and Learning* (2014) examines how teachers teach, how students learn, and the gap in between. Her writing and reading workshop model and Atwell's own classroom experiences help teachers understand more deeply what really works when teaching adolescents.

WHEN KIDS CAN'T READ: WHAT TEACHERS CAN DO

What do you do when you are teaching English at the secondary level and your kids can't read? This question is what led Kyleen Beers (2003) to write her book, which not only helps readers improve their skills, but empowers them to improve their confidence and attitudes. When teaching middle school, this inspiring book was Michelle's "bible." It aided her immensely in understanding how to teach comprehension, fluency, vocabulary, and decoding skills.

DEEPER READING: COMPREHENDING CHALLENGING TEXTS, 4-12

Kelly Gallagher has taught high school English in Anaheim, California, for more than 20 years and doesn't just theorize about what makes great teaching; he actually practices it. This book (2004) helps teachers of grades 4-12 when they notice their students are just giving reading a cursory glance or are comprehending at a surface level. Not only does it show teachers how students can more deeply comprehend and connect with more difficult texts, it also provides guidance to help teach at that level. As with all of Gallagher's books, it's full of real-life classroom stories and practical ideas for helping students read beyond the surface.

WRITE LIKE THIS: TEACHING REAL-WORLD WRITING THROUGH MODELING AND MENTOR TEXTS

This is another helpful book by Kelly Gallagher (2011). He believes that, if you want to learn how to write well, you must notice what successful writers do and then do it yourself. Thus, his model of teaching comes from writing himself and choosing exemplary mentor texts for his students to read and use. As most writing teachers know, emulating good writing elevates students' writing and moves them into a world where writing is important regardless of career path.

COMPREHENSION AND COLLABORATION: INQUIRY CIRCLES FOR CURIOSITY, ENGAGEMENT, AND UNDERSTANDING

In the winter of 2015, Michelle watched "Smokey" Daniels present a day-long workshop centered around this book (2015), and was hooked. She immediately pre-ordered it and went to work as a coach encouraging staff members at her school to let her try some of the ideas out on their kids. It's messy and can be time-consuming, but nothing is better than watching and listening to students share opinions, ask questions, and gracefully and politely spark debate around important issues and topics. This book has everything you need to help manage a classroom where your students research, collaborate, and comprehend topics in all content areas. Additionally, Harvey and Daniels have correlated much of the work in this book to common state and national standards.

STRATEGIES THAT WORK: TEACHING COMPREHENSION FOR ENGAGEMENT, UNDERSTANDING, AND BUILDING KNOWLEDGE

Harvey and Goudvis originally released this book over a decade ago, and in the third edition (2017), they offer new perspectives on helping students become engaged and independent readers. The book has been a much-used and appreciated guide for teachers of reading everywhere.

CONTENT PLANNING: MATHEMATICS

MATHEMATICAL MINDSETS

Through her book, *Mathematical Mindsets* (2015) and companion Youcubed.org website, Stanford University professor Jo Boaler has achieved something akin to a rock star status in the world of mathematics education in recent years. Boaler uses an extensive research base to dispel myths about math ability and goes on to recommend specific instructional practices that encourage positive beliefs about all students' potential for math achievement. Strategies outlined include: low-floor high-ceiling tasks that are accessible and extendable, number talks, visualization, cooperative group work, and establishing positive norms for math classes. The low-floor high-ceiling tasks in particular are so popular and energizing among students and teachers that Boaler followed up by co-writing several books offering up tasks and games at each grade level (for grades 3 through 7 as of this writing).

In *Visible Learning for Mathematics, Grades K-12* (2016), Hattie et al. provide a synthesis of research-based practices that lead to higher levels of achievement in mathematics. They describe various strategies but also go beyond that to make the point that it is not necessarily the strategy itself that is crucial so much as the timing of the strategy. It's about choosing the right strategy at the right time depending on where learners are within three phases of learning: Surface, Deep, and Transfer. After writing this book, the authors developed four helpful classroom companions, one for primary grades (k-2), one for grades 3-5, one for grades 6-8, and one for high school.

The Five Practices in Practice (2019) is a much anticipated follow up to a book by Smith and Sherin that was published by the National Council for Teachers of Mathematics (Smith & Stein 2018). It outlines five research-based practices that are designed to increase the quality and accessibility of constructive math discussion: Anticipating, Monitoring, Selecting, Sequencing, and Connecting. The authors use ample examples from the classroom to illustrate and clarify the practices in action.

Sousa's *How the Brain Learns Mathematics* (2014) describes the cognitive mechanisms for learning mathematics at various developmental levels and presents brain-friendly strategies for overcoming math difficulties and support learning for all students, such as the concrete-representational-abstract approach to developing conceptual understanding.

This section was contributed by Ellen Dorsey, Mathematics Instructional Coach with Washington Central Advisory Union 32 in Burlington, Vermont.

In *Solving for Why* (2012), Tapper describes strategies for diagnosing and remediating math difficulties by developing and testing theories using a three-frame approach. The book goes on to describe and recommend math menu as a strategy that can be used to design effective instruction for all learners in diverse math classrooms. The index is filled with examples at multiple grade levels.

FORMATIVE ASSESSMENT

STUDENT-INVOLVED CLASSROOM ASSESSMENT

When Jim was a student of Michael Fullan's at the University of Toronto, he once asked Michael whom he should talk to in order to learn about how to improve schools. One of the first people Michael named was Rick Stiggins. Not long after that, Jim found himself in Rick's office, trying to learn as much as possible as Rick generously shared his time and ideas.

The book that has most influenced our thinking at ICG is Stiggins' Student-Involved Classroom Assessment (2000), but several other books by Stiggins and his team have also been helpful. In particular, Jan Chappuis' *Seven Strategies of Assessment for Learning 2nd Edition* (2014) is an accessible and helpful book about the topic. An additional useful and frequently used book on formative assessment is Wiliam and Leahy's *Embedded Formative Assessment* (2018), which explains how formative assessment methods should be integrated into daily teaching practices. The authors summarize relevant research and explain how teachers should use strategies such as learning intentions, success criteria, feedback, collaborative and cooperative learning, and self-regulated learning to increase student achievement.

STUDENT ENGAGEMENT

CHAMPS: A PROACTIVE AND POSITIVE APPROACH TO CLASSROOM MANAGEMENT

Few people have had a greater impact on our work than Randy Sprick. In fact, his influence is so great on our thinking that he was awarded ICG's Don Deshler Leadership Award in 2015. Sprick's book *CHAMPS: A Proactive and Positive Approach to Classroom Management* (2009) is an essential book for teams that want to include classroom management strategies in their playbook. Phillip Schlechty's *Engaging Students: The New Level of Working on the Work* (2011) has especially helped us define different kinds of engagement. Schlechty distinguishes between engagement, strategic compliance, ritualistic compliance, retreatism, and rebellion.

ENGAGEMENT BY DESIGN & ENGAGING CHILDREN: IGNITING A DRIVE FOR DEEPER LEARNING

We have found two other books to be very helpful. Fisher, Frye, and Quaglia's *Engagement by Design* (2017) also clarifies the definition of engagement and provides many helpful strategies for increasing behavioral and cognitive engagement. A special feature of the book is the inclusion of results from Quaglia's Student Voice survey, which reveals conclusively how important it is to increase engagement. Additionally, Ellin Oliver Keene's *Engaging Children: Igniting a Drive for Deeper Learning* (2018) further expands our understanding of engagement, shares powerful strategies, and, what we might like best, shares the opinions of students on engagement.

TEACH LIKE A PIRATE: INCREASE STUDENT ENGAGEMENT, BOOST YOUR CREATIVITY, AND TRANSFORM YOUR LIFE AS AN EDUCATOR

Finally, Dave Burgess's *Teach Like a Pirate: Increase Student Engagement, Boost Your Creativity, and Transform Your Life as an Educator* (2012) is a highly engaging combination of inspirational ideas about the importance of teachers being passionate, enthusiastic (even if they have to fake until they make it), and skillful at building rapport with students. Additionally, Burgess outlines many instructional hooks teachers can use (such as the kinesthetic hook, which describes how to incorporate movement into a lesson, and the interior design hook, which is about adjusting the lighting, look, spatial arrangement, and so forth, of a classroom to create a better atmosphere for learning) to increase engagement in the classroom.

Frequently Asked Questions

In the two years since the publication of *The Impact Cycle* (Knight, 2017), we have fielded many questions about the creation, revision, and dissemination of playbooks from coaches all over the world. This section provides answers to the most common questions that coaches ask as they create playbooks for their coaching practice. That said, we always reinforce the Partnership Principle of praxis— that professionals decide for themselves what works for them and their colleagues as they do the work of implementing something new. Coaches make the final call on what constitutes a playbook that works best.

Q: Who creates the playbook?

A: The primary creators of a playbook are instructional coaches; they need ownership of the instructional playbook based on what they know deeply and can explain clearly. Some district personnel may be included in the creation of the playbook as the coaches examine the alignment of the playbook with the district's mission, vision, and initiatives. Inclusion of more people can lead to more ideas, more thoroughness, and more buy-in, but including more people can also lead to a drop-off in efficiency, and if a lot of people are involved, the primary users of the playbook, instructional coaches, may end up with a playbook that is not exactly what they need.

Q: How large should the playbook be?

A: To answer this question, we use the phrase "lean and clean." The playbook must be usable. If it's too big and cumbersome, it's not usable. The playbook is focused on the strategies that address the PEERS goals that the teachers most often set with coaches.

Q: How do we structure the playbook?

A: The playbook consists of three main areas: the Table of Contents, the One-Page Description, and Checklists. This minimal structure is intended to help coaches keep the playbook as simple (and thus as usable) as possible. See Chapter 1 for more information.

Q: Should the playbook take the form of a paper document or a digital document?

A: We believe it's best to have both versions to address individual teacher preferences with the following caveats. Digital copies work if the coach is not sharing the strategies face-to-face. If you use a digital format, ensure that any internal links to other pages or documents work. Maintaining a paper copy of the playbook is also a good idea because the uncertainty of some school Wi-Fi systems may limit access to the playbook at unpredictable times unless the coach has a paper copy of it at hand. Not having access to the playbook during a coaching conversation is frustrating for both the coach and the teacher.

Q: What is the clearest way to organize the playbook for readability?

A: The Table of Contents is the first page of the playbook (see CHAPTER 2). Each strategy's One-Pager (see CHAPTER 3) appears in the order in which the strategy appears in the Table of Contents. Each checklist for a specific strategy (see CHAPTER 4) appears immediately after its One-Pager. We've outlined an example Table of Contents on the next page.

TABLE OF CONTENTS (LISTING STRATEGIES 1-15)

Strategy 1

» One-Pager

   » Checklist A

   » Checklist B

Strategy 2

» One-Pager

   » Checklist A

   » Checklist B

Strategy 3

» One-Pager

   » Checklist A

   » Checklist B

   » Checklist C

... and so forth.

A playbook should be custom-designed for the setting where it will be used, so those who are designing it should not feel restricted by this proposed structure. If a better structure emerges for your school or district, use it.

Q: Should a school system create one playbook for the entire district, one per grade level/content area, or one per individual coach?

A: This is a tricky question. If there are several coaches in a district, there can be a common district playbook consisting of the highest-impact strategies that align with district initiatives. Coaches can then individualize it based on the goals their teachers set. Playbook strategies are based on good pedagogy, and these strategies are implemented differently based on age-appropriateness, for example. See Chapter 2 for more information.

Having a playbook that is consistent across a district is helpful because each coach can share what he or she is learning about implementation, and everyone can attend the same professional development for the same strategies. But even a consistent

HELPFUL HINT

Always include page numbers both on the Table of Contents and the playbook itself for easy reference.

playbook is not helpful if it does not meet the needs of a school, teacher, or students, so some customization may be needed.

Q: Once the coach has shared strategies with the teacher for a particular goal, does the teacher still need to read and research those strategies?

A: Teachers can decide whether to do more research or reading around strategies. More research cannot hurt. Coaches have a depth of strategy knowledge that can save the teacher time, but we never discourage teachers who want to learn more from doing so.

Q: Once the playbook draft is complete, does the coach have to continue to read and research additional strategies?

A: One of the coach's responsibilities is to continually deepen his or her knowledge of current research around high-impact strategies. The deeper the coach's knowledge, the richer the conversation and the clearer the description for the teacher. It is difficult to teach what you don't know deeply. Furthermore, as researchers learn more, coaches need to be learning and sharing that information. Coaches are curators of knowledge, who share the best practices in a school, so they should always be learning, and their playbooks are therefore never "finished."

Q: Does every teacher receive a complete copy of the coach's playbook?

A: The playbook is truly a coach's tool. Coaches share it provisionally and dialogically in coaching conversations regarding PEERS goals. The intent is not to hand the teacher a list of strategies (which teachers may perceive as very directive); instead, the playbook is intended to serve as a reference for high-impact strategies that coaches know deeply and can explain clearly. Nevertheless, we don't think the playbook should be withheld from people who are interested; rather, we have found that it works best when used as a response to the student-focused goals identified by teachers.

Q: How should coaches share the playbook with teachers?

A: Dialogically, in conversation with the teacher when setting PEERS goals, usually during the Identify phase of *The Impact Cycle*. The teacher and coach typically work on the checklists during the Learn phase of *The Impact Cycle* before, during, and after modeling as the teacher practices using the strategy while working on the PEERS goal.

Q: Should the playbook include all of the strategies that a school system has been exposed to in professional development sessions?

A: Probably not. The playbook includes strategies for PEERS goals in the areas where teachers most often request coaching assistance. If, for example, the school system is involved in a major shift with regard to safety drill procedures, staff members may receive a great deal of training in those procedures. If teachers are frequently requesting coaching support in school safety, strategies from those trainings may be in the playbook; if teachers are not requesting that kind of assistance, then those strategies would not be included in the playbook.

Q: Is the playbook "carved in stone"?

A: No. Definitely not! A playbook is a living document that needs regular review and revision based on what is used and what is not used and reflects coaches' deepening knowledge and the PEERS goals their teachers are setting.

Q: What is the process for revising the playbook?

A: Coaches need a periodic, established process for meeting to discuss revisions to the playbook. We suggest those meetings occur at least quarterly. Some questions might be as follows:

» Do we need additional high-impact strategies in any areas?
» Do we have strategies that are rarely or never used that we can delete from the playbook?
» Are our checklists clear and complete? Have teachers made changes to them that we may consider changing on the master checklist?

See Chapters 2, 3, and 4 for specific guidelines on revising each section of the playbook.

Q: Can coaches use checklists that they did not create themselves?

HELPFUL HINT

Since the playbook is a living document, it is important to include revision dates to help everyone with access to the playbook know when a section was most recently revised.

A: Yes. Coaches do not need to reinvent the wheel. They can begin with a checklist that is part of a curricular document or was written by another coach and then make changes to it as the need arises. Coaches need to examine checklists for accuracy and clarity, but that's part of the power of the conversation between the teacher and coach. The teacher gives input, which increases ownership.

Q: And what else?

A: Coaches often have questions about the organization, communication, and distribution of the playbook and its strategies. We have tried to answer the most common questions here to assist coaches in navigating those issues as they arise.

Change leaders may wish to gather the playbook design team together before creating the playbook so that the team members can ask questions about the playbook and its use. Whoever leads the discussion can use the questions and answers included here to answer as many of their questions as is helpful. The more clarity everyone has on the process of creating the playbook and the role it plays in coaching, the more focused everyone will be when actually working on building one.

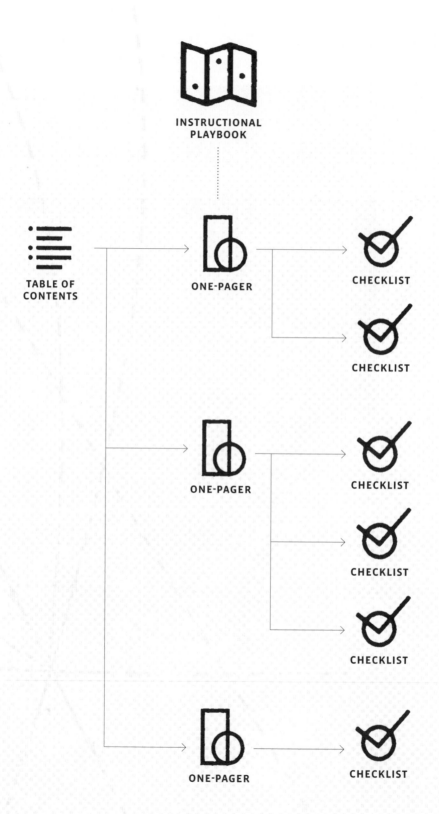

INSTRUCTIONAL PLAYBOOK

TABLE OF CONTENTS

ONE-PAGER

CHECKLIST

CHECKLIST

ONE-PAGER

CHECKLIST

CHECKLIST

CHECKLIST

ONE-PAGER

CHECKLIST

Sample Playbooks

In the previous section, we addressed all of the most commonly asked questions we receive about the playbook, except for the most common question of all: "Can I see more examples of playbooks?" We are fortunate that several of the school systems with whom we have partnered over the past two years have allowed us to use segments of their playbooks for that purpose.

On the following pages, we have excerpted playbooks from 5 different districts. The excerpts are only examples of how individual districts have approached their playbooks and can serve as inspiration and support as our readers embark on creating their own playbooks. Each of the following examples were pulled from full playbooks. *We have isolated particular elements of each playbook so that readers may see different ways of constructing a playbook.* We caution against viewing these examples as officially "ICG sanctioned" playbooks, or as the only ways that one can approach developing a playbook. In fact, as you read the information about each district that appears before their playbook excerpt, you'll see that each of these four districts modified the process and/or the product as necessary to meet their needs.

IRVING ISD, IRVING, TEXAS

Irving Independent School District (ISD) sits in a suburb just west of Dallas, Texas. Serving 34,000 students, Irving ISD is ethnically and economically diverse, and 80% of their families are designated as economically disadvantaged. Jana Claxton and Kristina Feldner began working on their playbook in earnest in 2018 after attending a session on creating an instructional playbook at the Instructional Coaching Group's (ICG) annual Teaching Learning Coaching Conference in 2017.

The creation of Irving ISD's playbook was a highly collaborative process in which just over 100 stakeholders dove into the work in an ICG-facilitated session. Their draft then went to a smaller group for refinement and came back again to the large group for customization.

Jana and Kristina like the playbook because it keeps strategy information lean and "digestible." They also believe that its multiple iterations during its development have reminded people to "always keep a focus on high-impact strategies." Although creating the playbook has been an undertaking that has taken time, Jana and Kristina both highly recommend that "everyone try it."

This excerpt of the 2018-2019 Irving ISD Instructional Playbook is reprinted with permission of the Irving Independent School District, Irving, Texas. ©2018 Irving Independent School District.

Table of Contents

Content Planning
PLC Q1: What do we want students to know and be able to do?
- Lesson Cycle
- Purposeful Planning

Instruction
- Effective Questioning
- Cooperative Learning
- Academic Conversations
- Critical Thinking
- Reading & Writing Across the Curriculum

Assessment for Learning (Formative Assessment) (Q2 PLC)
PLC Q2: How will we know that students have learned it?
- Pre-assessment
- Checks for Understanding
- Effective Feedback
- Reflection of Instruction based on Student Learning
- Student Self-assessment
- Rubrics for Mastery

Community Building
- Positive Classroom Environment
- Relationship Building
- Classroom Management

Rev. 10.15.18

TABLE OF CONTENTS

ONE-PAGER

CHECKLIST

Lesson Cycle

In One Sentence
- A lesson cycle is a method to structure a lesson in an intentional manner to maximize student learning.

The Hattie Check
- Planning and prediction 0.76; Deliberate practice 0.79; Teacher clarity 0.75

What's the Point?
- Various components work together to develop the content, topic, and student learning and all aspects of the lesson cycle are well planned, aligned, and timely.
- Adequate modeling and guidance is provided to support students at varying points in the lesson.
- Deliberate openings and closings are utilized to clarify the objective, assess student learning, instruction and misconceptions.
- Purposeful opportunities for technology integration are embedded to increase student engagement and effectively differentiate for students of all learning styles.

How is the Lesson Cycle used by Teachers?
- Introduce (engage or hook) and close out your lesson (closing task or exit ticket)
- Activate student prior knowledge, vocabulary, and/or schema
- Allow student feedback on how the lesson was taught and what they learned
- Use models of strong and weak samples of class work

How is the Lesson Cycle used by Students?
- Lessons are organized or chunked in a way that students can understand.
- Students understand objective and how it can be applied to their life.
- Students can reteach lessons to their peers and have academic conversation.
- Students benefit from structured time management that maximizes their production through a class period.
- Students can use technology to enrich their understanding.

Content Connections
- MATH (Engage, Explore, Summarize)
- ELAR (Gradual Release)
- SS (Engage, Explore, Summarize)
- Science (5E)

Content Planning
PLC Q1: What do we want students to know and be able to do?

Rev. 10.15.18

TABLE OF CONTENTS

ONE-PAGER

CHECKLIST

✓ CHECKLIST: Lesson Closure

	✓
Develop a summary of the days learning to share during your lesson closing. Teacher and students connect the learning objective to other areas, to the real world, and to students' lives	
Students might share solutions, challenges, and/or discoveries. Teacher & students celebrate multiple approaches that led to a shared, accurate understanding	
Utilize your guiding questions to check for understanding at the end of your class daily	
Use a timer to stop instruction/activities with 5 minutes remaining	
Academic vocabulary is defined and posted on a Word Wall and/or anchor chart	

Content Planning
PLC Q1: What do we want students to know and be able to do?

Rev. 10.15.18

TABLE OF CONTENTS

ONE-PAGER

CHECKLIST

Academic Conversation

In One Sentence
- **Academic conversations** are dialogues in which students focus on a topic and explore it by building, challenging, and negotiating relevant ideas.

The Hattie Check
- Classroom discussion = .82
- Research articles reported a high effect size for time on task comparing individualistic learning to cooperative learning (1.17) and achievement (.67).

What's the Point?
- Allowing students to discuss content verbally will help build language, knowledge, and understanding of material. Communicating your learning can aid in retaining information.
- Rich academic conversations can be powerful tools in schools to build:
  - literacy skills such as oral language and communication skills and inner dialogue
  - academic language and skills for negotiating meaning on a focused topic
  - critical thinking skills, creativity, engagement, and motivation
  - empathetic relationships and the understanding of different perspectives
  - the ability to cultivate connections and to build content understandings

How are Academic Conversations used by Teachers?
- Teachers use academic conversations--
  - to create student-centered learning opportunities
  - to formatively assess learning in real time through teacher observation and various digital platforms
  - to build academic vocabulary, language skills and structures
- To meet the needs of diverse and special needs learners through the practice of a variety of communication skills.
- To support the social/emotional development of learners through the structures, frequency, and purposes of communication.

How are Academic Conversations used by Students?
Students use academic conversations--
- to learn from peers through classroom and/or web-based interaction and problem solving
- to practice listening and speaking across content areas
- to clarify learning and provide opportunities for new thinking
- to explore unique perspectives, support ideas and provoke critical thinking

Instruction

Rev. 10.15.18

TABLE OF CONTENTS

ONE-PAGER

CHECKLIST

✓ CHECKLIST: Planning and Execution

	✓
Identify the knowledge and big ideas students need to learn.	
Create the most effective kind, type, and level of questions.	
Determine the outcome students need to produce at the end of the conversation.	
Develop and provide sentence stems for student use to sustain the conversation.	
Promote dialogue by listening to students' key ideas and restating them clearly when students' comments lack focus.	
Suggest connections between ideas offered by students and support synthesis of new information into students' schema.	
Provide time for students to reflect on the conversation and develop the expected product.	

✓ CHECKLIST: Culture & Expectations

	✓
Purposefully group students and determined the response structure	
Students clearly understand the learning objective	
Establish students norms and expectations for how to act, talk, and move during the academic conversation	
Modeling and scaffolding the interpretation of visual aids, pictorials, and graphical representations during academic conversations for all learners	
Listen with empathy and encourage students by frequently offering authentic praise and recognition for their efforts	
Promote dialogue by listening for students' key ideas	
Restate student ideas clearly when their comments lack focus	
Teachers and students suggest connections between ideas offered to increase the level of thinking in the academic conversation.	

Student Self-Assessment

In One Sentence
- Students self-assess their progress towards learning targets so they can make adjustments to their learning.

The Hattie Check
- Student expectation = 1.44; student self-questioning = 0.64

What's the Point?
- Student self-assessment is a powerful strategy for students to employ to increase their learning outcomes by becoming aware of what they do or think they understand and what they don't understand or is unclear.
- Students become aware of their learning by employing a form of self-questioning on their academic performance.
- Reflection on learning increases student engagement, critical thinking skills, and learning outcomes.

How is student reflection of learning used by Teachers?
- Teachers need to facilitate student reflection at planned checkpoints to help the student monitor and adjust their understanding.
- Teachers use the results of student reflection to identify areas of instructional need and adjust the delivery of teaching.

How is student reflection of learning used by Students?
- Student needs to be knowledgeable of what they will reflect on before, during and after the lesson.
- Students can check for understanding by self assessing their learning using a self-assessment tool.
- Students can reflect on their learning in cooperative groups by questioning each other and providing feedback.
- Student reflection at planned checkpoints helps the student monitor and adjust their progress.

Assessment FOR Learning
PLC Q2: How will we know that students have learned it?

Rev. 10.15.18

TABLE OF CONTENTS

ONE-PAGER

CHECKLIST

✓ CHECKLIST: Success Criteria

	✓
Learning target is clear to the students.	
Teacher selects or creates a self reflection tool for students to become: aware of learning and growth, and responsible for learning.	
Student needs to be aware of the self reflection tool.	
Teacher teaches/models the use of the self reflective questioning by using the gradual release model.	
Teacher provides choice of self reflection tools.	

Assessment FOR Learning
PLC Q2: How will we know that students have learned it?

Rev. 10.15.18

TABLE OF CONTENTS

ONE-PAGER

CHECKLIST

Positive Classroom Environment

In One Sentence:
- A positive classroom environment is a community of shared trust between teachers and students where students are allowed to take risks and feel safe.

The Hattie Check:
- Teacher-student relationships = .72; Classroom behavioral = .68; Classroom management = .52 (while the overall size effect is .52, it should be noted that in classrooms where there is a great need for management strategies, the impact would exceed the effect of .52)

What's the Point?
- A positive environment is one in which students feel a sense of belonging, trust others, and feel encouraged to tackle challenges, take risks, and ask questions (Bucholz & Sheffler, 2009).
- Such an environment provides relevant content, clear learning goals and feedback, opportunities to build social skills, and strategies to help students succeed (Weimer, 2009).

What Can Teachers Do to Create a Positive Classroom Environment?
- Teachers are knowledgeable of their students' backgrounds and their social, emotional, and academic needs [English language learners, students with IEPs, 504 students, students protected by the Vento Act (homeless), Gifted and Talented].
- Teachers should design a learner-friendly environment.
- Teachers should model building positive relationships with students to show them how to build positive relationships with each other.

How Can Students Have a Say in the Classroom Environment?
- Students are aware of the needs of their peers and learn to support and value each other.
- Students can be asked to help with the design of the classroom to establish a learner-friendly environment.
- Students feel comfortable asking questions and taking risks in a positive classroom environment to promote their learning.

TABLE OF CONTENTS

ONE-PAGER

CHECKLIST

✓ CHECKLIST: Classroom Norms & Procedures

	✓
Introduce and define social norms as vocabulary with examples	
Ask students what is ideal learning environment	
Gather input from all students in writing, in a visible location	
Generate a list of norms together, combining similar idea	
Write less than five norms on an anchor chart and have all students and teacher sign	
Post chart in the classroom, and consistently refer to and reevaluate the norms	

✓ CHECKLIST: Culturally Responsive Strategy

To Create Learner-Friendly Cultures	✓
Conduct Student Interviews	
Co-construct norms with students	
Positively reinforce students when they act consistently within cultural norms	
Use curriculum/materials from various and relevant cultures	
Provide opportunities for students to consider culturally different points of view through student dialogue and interaction	
Use purposeful and varied grouping strategies (homogenous, and heterogenous) to promote cultural growth	
Allow students a choice in creating authentic work	

TABLE OF CONTENTS

ONE-PAGER

CHECKLIST

✓ CHECKLIST: Creating a Social Contract

	✓
Greet students in a positive manner.	
Explain your role as the teacher.	
Explain what a social contract is and how it will function in your classroom.	
Guide students into a conversation regarding social norms within the classroom environment.	
Make social contract visible.	
Students acknowledge and sign the social contract.	
Redirect by reinforcing and referring to the social contract as needed.	

Community Building

Rev. 10.15.18

TABLE OF CONTENTS

ONE-PAGER

CHECKLIST

RACHEL LEFORCE, INSTRUCTIONAL COACH, OKLAHOMA CITY PUBLIC SCHOOLS, OKLAHOMA CITY, OKLAHOMA

Oklahoma City Public Schools (OKPS) is an urban district in Oklahoma City, Oklahoma. OKPS is the largest district in Oklahoma and serves more than 46,000 students, 84% of whom come from economically disadvantaged home environments. Rachel LeForce, is an OKPS instructional coach at Kaiser Elementary.

Rachel started with input from ICG's workshop around the instructional playbook as well as looking to Jim's instructional playbook in The Impact Cycle and the district's work with Robert Marzano's The Art and Science of Teaching framework. Rachel used the "Big Four" structure from High-Impact Instruction to help make the playbook more manageable. Rachel tells us that the creation of the playbook has definitely been an advantage when sharing and using it with teachers.

Rachel uses the playbook as part of the Impact Cycle, and she worked hard to align the strategies to the goals that teachers most commonly set in Impact Cycles. Additionally, Rachel mentions the benefits of having checklists to help with the district-encouraged Marzano framework.

Creating and using a playbook has helped Rachel expand her knowledge about high-leverage strategies, especially when coaching a teacher in a grade level outside of her expertise and/or experience. Rachel tells us that the playbook "has really helped me be more well-rounded with regard to instruction and has helped me solidify my range of competencies."

This excerpt from Rachel LeForce's instructional playbook is reprinted with permission of the Oklahoma City Public Schools, Oklahoma City, Oklahoma. ©2018 Oklahoma City Public Schools.

Rachel LeForce's Coaching Playbook
Table of Contents

Instructional Strategies
- Independent Practice
  Checklists: Gradual Release, Workstations
- Learning Objectives
  Checklist: Writing Objectives, Objectives in the Classroom,
- Previewing/Advanced Organizers(AO)
  Checklist: AO-Expository, AO-Narrative, Skimming, KWL

Classroom Climate
- Engagement- Questioning
  Checklists: Wait Time, Response Cards, Response Chaining
- Rules and Procedures
  Checklist: Explicit Teaching, Suggested Areas, CHAMPS, Class Meeting
- Positive Reinforcement
  Checklist: 5 to 1 Ratio, Tangible Recognition, Home Recognition

Planning
- Standards Based Planning
  Checklists: Planning with End in Mind, Guiding Questions
- Learning Maps
  Checklist: Creation, Classroom Use
- Planning for Declarative Knowledge
  Checklist: Initial Learning, Extending and Applying
- Planning for Procedural Knowledge
  Checklist: Initial Learning, Extending and Applying

Assessment
- Formative
  Checklist: Data Notebooks, Exit Ticket, 3-2-1 Countdown
- Summative
  Checklist: Reading Record, Data Review Protocol, Benchmark Literacy End of Unit
  Assessments

TABLE OF CONTENTS

ONE-PAGER

CHECKLIST

Classroom Instruction
Previewing/Advanced Organizers

In One Sentence: Previewing is any activity that starts students thinking about content that is about to be taught as well as promotes making connections between new and previously covered content.

Marzano Connection: According to *The Art and Science of Teaching* a study done by Walberg in 1999 there is an average effect size of .45 or a 17% gain.

What's the Point?:
- To promote interest and curiosity about upcoming lesson or unit
- To make connections between prior knowldge and what is to be learned
- To provide a glimpse or summary into upcoming content
- To provide a framework for upcoming objectives
- To communicate what is important about upcoming learning

How Previewing is used by Teachers:
- Teachers use to see and hear what students may already know
- Teachers use to point out connections to previously presented content
- Teachers use to ask questions to activate prior knowledge and curiosity
- Teachers use to provide summary of upcoming learning

How Previewing is used by Students:
- Students use to connect new content with past content
- Students use to activate prior knowledge or related knowledge
- Students use for skimming printed material
- Students use for review of prepared notes

Advanced Organizer/Expository	✔	Comments/Evidence
State a description of the new content		
Connect description to current objective		
Highlight important content		
Connect to previously covered content		

Advanced Organizer/Narrative	✔	Comments/Evidence
State personal experience or real world event		
Connect experience or event to upcoming content		
Connect experience or event to current objective		
Connect to previously covered content		

Advanced Organizer/Skimming	✓	Comments/Evidence
Provide student with printed material		
Students read section heading		
Students read all subheadings with one or two of the first sentences		
Review illustrations, graphs, and charts		
Students summarize what they think the passage will be about		
Teacher links student summaries with previously covered content		
Teacher links student summaries with upcoming content and current objective		

TABLE OF CONTENTS

ONE-PAGER

CHECKLIST

Graphic Advanced Organizer/KWL	✔	Comments/Evidence
Create chart with section for Know, Want to Know, Learned (can be whole class or individual student recording form)		
Share topic or brief description of upcoming content		
Connect topic to current objective and previously covered content		
Students brainstorm words, and phrases that relate to the topic and record in the "K: column		
Teachers asks students what they want to know about this topic and they record in the "W" column		
While participating in the learning activity students should be looking for the answers to the questions in the "W" column		
After learning activity record found answers and new understandings in the "L" column		

TABLE OF CONTENTS

ONE-PAGER

CHECKLIST

Classroom Climate
Positive Reinforcement

In One Sentence: Positive reinforcement is any action (verbal, tangible, peer) that increases the likelihood that a behavior will reoccur

Marzano Connection: According to *The Art and Science of Teaching* reinforcement decreases inappropriate behavior by an average effect size of -.86 or 31%

What's the Point:
- To replace inappropriate behavior with appropriate behavior
- To promote adherence to rules and procedures
- To crease a classroom climate conducive to learning

How is positive reinforcement used by Teachers:
- Teachers use positive verbal comments to acknowledge adherence to expectations
- Teachers use tangible reinforcements to acknowledge adherence to expectations
- Teachers use to positive social pressures that promote adherence to expectations
- Teachers use to promote a positive classroom climate

How is positive reinforcement used by Students:
- Students use acknowledgement to enhance learned behaviors
- Students use social pressures to adhere to expected behaviors
- Students use acknowledgements as a tool for learning appropriate classroom behaviors.

TABLE OF CONTENTS

ONE-PAGER

CHECKLIST

5 to 1 ratio of positive to corrective classroom comments	✓	Comments/Evidence
Brainstorm phrases for behavior specific responses		
Meet students at the door		
Write specific behaviors you want to see in the classroom on sticky notes- state and pass out during class time		
Create tool to track positive comments in a designated amount to time		

Tangible Recognitions	✔	Comments/Evidence
Has established token system (PBIS rewards, Class Dojo, Class Point System)		
Has established procedures for how and why points are given		
Has established reflection process to determine if points are being given in an equitable manner		
Has menu or store where points can be exchanged for nominal reward or certificate of recognition		
Has established schedule for exchanging points		
Develops plan for decreasing use of tangible recognitions when class behavior goals are being met		

Home Recognitions	✔	Comments/Evidence
Be specific about behavior being recognized		
Encourage home adult to communicate to the student about your positive recognition		
Phone Calls		
Establish schedule for making positive calls home		
Establish protocol for when you are unable to reach an adult from home		
Emails		
Establish a schedule for sending positive emails of recognition		
Establish a template or general guidelines for positive emails		
Notes		
Will you use hand written notes or premade certificates?		

TABLE OF CONTENTS

ONE-PAGER

CHECKLIST

Planning
Standards Based Planning

In One Sentence: Standards based planning insures that classroom instruction is based on instructional standards and that the assessments, and learning experiences promote the mastery of those standards

Marzano Connection: According to *The Art and Science of Teaching* a study done by Blumenfeld & Meece complex, well-designed tasks facilitate deeper levels of learning and higher engagement

What's the Point:
- To have a clear understanding of the intended outcomes of instruction
- To develop instruction that promotes mastery of standards
- To promote high expectations for all students
- To provide platform for differentiation

How is standards based planning used by Teachers:
- Teachers use to write objectives to prepare students for instruction
- Teachers use to design pre-assessments to guide instruction
- Teachers use to design learning experiences that promote mastery of standards
- Teachers use to collect evidence of learning

How standards based planning used by Students:
- Students use to prepare for learning new content, skills, and procedures
- Students use to set goals for meeting standards
- Students use to interact with new content
- Students use to practice new skills and procedures

TABLE OF CONTENTS

ONE-PAGER

CHECKLIST

Planning with the end in Mind	✔	Comments
Identify Desired Results		
Analyze standards		
Identify the essentials standards		
Determine Acceptable Evidence		
Identify assessment criteria		
Identify/design assessment format		
Determine modifications and accommodations		
Plan Learning Experiences		
Pre-assessment		
Anticipatory Set		
Objective/Purpose		
Input		
Modeling		
Check for Understanding		
Guided Practice		
Independent Practice		

TABLE OF CONTENTS

ONE-PAGER

CHECKLIST

Guiding Questions for Units	✔	Comments
Questions for procedural knowledge needed to meet standards		
Questions for content knowledge needed to meet standards		
Need a range of DOK questions		
Directs the path to learning goals		
Provides coordination of unit		

TABLE OF CONTENTS

ONE-PAGER

CHECKLIST

FRISCO ISD PLAYBOOK, FRISCO, TEXAS

The Frisco Independent School District (ISD) is in Frisco, Texas, a suburb north of Dallas. For the past five years, Frisco ISD has been one of the fastest growing districts in the nation. As of early 2019, Frisco had more than 60,000 students who have historically been largely ethnically homogenous, but their 42 elementary schools are increasingly diverse. Mary Webb is the Director of Elementary Education in Frisco, and she works with one dedicated instructional coach per elementary school and 7 content coordinators who are housed at the central office and support the instructional coaches. They started their coaching program in 2012 and began working with ICG in 2017.

The beginning stages of creating Frisco ISD's instructional playbook began in March 2018 with content coordinators and special programs coordinators (who facilitate the English language learners/bilingual, special education, and dyslexia programs). The team started with the strategies that were universally the "most important and aligned to our work," according to Mary. The draft of the playbook then went to coaches in the Fall of 2018 for revisions and continues to be a work in progress. "We had coaches asking for this, and we saw a great need for it," Mary reports.

Coaches use the playbook in their Impact Cycles as well as with the special education coaches. Mary stresses the benefit of the playbook transcending all content areas as well as the fact that it simplifies the steps for teachers. She also mentions the benefits of having a structure for the coaches to use as especially helpful. Frisco's high volume of growth also comes into play, Mary says, because "We are growing so fast that we are always adding new coaches, and we can't train them on all the strategies right away. [The playbook] provides a structure and specificity that they all have access to." Mary also mentions that some teachers have access to the playbook and have used it in their planning.

Playbook Table of Contents

Collaborative Planning
Data Analysis
Pacing
Content Planning

Instruction
Instructional Models
Instructional Strategies
Cooperative Learning

Assessment
Formative Assessment
Common Formative Assessments
Summative Assessments
Creating Rubrics

Community Building
Learner-Friendly Culture
Power With vs. Power Over
Expectations
Witness to the Good and Fluent Corrections

FRISCO
INDEPENDENT SCHOOL DISTRICT

TABLE OF CONTENTS

ONE-PAGER

CHECKLIST

Data Analysis

In One Sentence:
A process for analyzing data using analytical and logical reasoning to examine the results of student performance.

The Research Says:
- Hattie: Feedback = 0.75, Goals = 0.58, Response to Intervention = 1.29

What's the Point?
- Data Analysis allows teachers to develop and pursue measurable improvement goals that align with the standards.
- Data analysis allows teachers to discover strengths and weaknesses in their individual teaching in order to learn from each other.
- Data analysis allows teachers to determine whether instructional strategies and pacing were appropriate.

How is Data Analysis Used by Teachers?
- Teachers determine if Tier 1 instruction was effective.
- Teachers prioritize standards for celebrations and improvement.
- Teachers identify instructional strategies to meet the needs of their students.

How does Data Analysis benefit Students?
Students received systematic and timely interventions.

FRISCO
INDEPENDENT SCHOOL DISTRICT

TABLE OF CONTENTS

ONE-PAGER

CHECKLIST

✓ CHECKLIST: DATA ANALYSIS

	✓
Make note of the number of students in Tier 1, Tier 2, and Tier 3 based on predetermined criteria.	
Identify standards where performance is: • Below 50% • Between 51% and 84% • Above 85%	
Examine student work samples and/or assessment questions for the lowest performance standard.	
Unpack and create learning targets based on the lowest performance standard.	
Create a small group lesson plan aligned to the identified learning targets.	
Identify students who will receive targeted instruction.	

FRISCO
INDEPENDENT SCHOOL DISTRICT

TABLE OF CONTENTS

ONE-PAGER

CHECKLIST

Vocabulary

In one sentence:
- If students have knowledge of specific terms and build their academic language, they are able to discuss and debate their thinking.

The Research Says:
- Hattie: Vocabulary programs .62
- Stahl & Fairbanks 1986: direct vocabulary instruction on words related to content (effect size = .97)

What's the point?
- Vocabulary knowledge is a strong predictor of understanding across content area.
- Students comprehension will increase by 33 percentile points when vocabulary instruction focuses on specific words important to the content they are reading as opposed to words from high frequency lists. (Marzano)

How Teachers should select and teach vocabulary:
- Teachers should choose 4-6 words per week for the content being studied.
- Teachers should refer to to the state standards to be sure that vocabulary lessons keep students on track for learning.
- Vocabulary should never be taught in isolation.

What are some examples of direct vocabulary instruction?
- Marzano's Six Steps
- Designing of Interactive Word Walls
- Scanning
- Graphic Organizers

How is vocabulary used by students?
Students use vocabulary:
- To access content knowledge
- To make connections between what they are doing and the concepts being taught
- To use words fluently as they problem solve, engage in experiments, read about historical/ political events, and interpret literature.

FRISCO
INDEPENDENT SCHOOL DISTRICT

TABLE OF CONTENTS

ONE-PAGER

CHECKLIST

✓ CHECKLIST: MARZANO'S SIX STEPS TO BUILDING ACADEMIC VOCABULARY

	✓
1 Teachers give students a description or explanation of the word or term using examples and visuals.	
2. Student give a description or explanation of a vocabulary word or term using their own words and record descriptions in their personal notebooks to reference later.	
3. Students draw a representation of the new vocabulary word or term.	
4. Students participate in activities that allow them to practice using the new words or terms.	
5. Students discuss the vocabulary words or terms as they work with partners, triads, or groups.	
6. Students participate in games that reinforce deep understanding of the new vocabulary words or terms	

✓ CHECKLIST: FRAYER MODEL

	✓
Student writes target vocabulary word or concept in center bubble.	
Student defines the target vocabulary words or concepts	
Apply this information by generating examples and non-examples	
Create a visual.	

FRISCO
INDEPENDENT SCHOOL DISTRICT

POUDRE SCHOOL DISTRICT, FT. COLLINS, COLORADO

Poudre School District serves just over 30,000 students in 50 schools in northern Colorado. Hilary Herrmann and a team of fellow coaches created their playbook after attending an ICG 5-day Intensive Institute in Lawrence, Kansas.

Hilary tells us that her team started the creation of their playbook by "casting a wide net" and looking at their district-adopted teaching rubric. After initially spending time focused on the rubric, they then "funneled it down." Hilary tells us at first there was some resistance, but once the team spent time discussing and creating the playbook, the resistance faded and her team was "all in."

Poudre's coaches use the playbook when working in Impact Cycles with teachers and have found the greatest benefits to be the checklists and having a specific structure that contributes to common language in their district. Although finding resources was originally one of the most challenging roadblocks, now that the playbook has been created, carving out time for revisions has also been challenging. Just as co-creating the playbook created commitment, Hilary knows that getting that same commitment from new coaches who weren't involved in its creation will take time and effort.

Since its creation, Poudre's playbook has become a valuable tool, especially when sharing it with teachers as a way to foster partnership in coaching conversations and to give teachers choices in addressing their goals for students.

This excerpt of the Poudre School District Instructional Playbook is reprinted with permission of the Poudre School District, Ft. Collins, Colorado. ©2018 Poudre School District.

Poudre School District Instructional Coach Playbook

Purpose	❏ Learning Targets ❏ Success Criteria ❏ Relevant & Transferrable Lesson Design

Assessment for Student Learning	❏ Formative Assessment Process
	    • Formative Feedback
	    • Collecting Evidence of Student Progress
	❏ Student Self-Assessment

Student Engagement	❏ Quality Questioning
	❏ Strategies that Capitalize on Learning Needs
	    • Discussion & Collaboration Routines
	    • Value Line
	    • Managed choice

Curriculum and Pedagogy	❏ Gradual Release of Responsibility
	❏ Thinking Strategies
	❏ Differentiated Instruction
	    • Differentiating Process
	    • Differentiating Product
	    • Differentiating Content

Classroom Environment and Culture	❏ Culturally Responsive Teaching
	    • Affirming Cultural Identities
	    • Fostering Positive Relationships
	    • Culturally Responsive Learning Environment
	    • Emphasizing Academic Growth
	    • Differentiating Instruction
	    • Consistent, Attentive Classroom Management
	    • Discussion and Collaboration Routines
	❏ Discussion and Collaboration Routines
	    • Turn to Your Neighbor
	    • Think, Pair, Share
	    • Jigsaw
	    • Round Table
	    • Value Line
	❏ Norms for Learning
	❏ Explicit Instruction of Rituals and Routines

June 2015 Playbook Drafting Team:
Theresa Burke, Instructional Coach, Bauder Elementary
Becca Benedict, Instructional Coach, Eyestone Elementary
Michelle Carey, Instructional Coach, Linton Elementary
Hilary Herrmann, Instructional Coach Coordinator
Mary Jane Raisley, Instructional Coach, Putnam Elementary
Eric Schmitz, English Language Acquisition Coach, Olander Elementary

TABLE OF CONTENTS

ONE-PAGER

CHECKLIST

Learning Target Guidelines

The purpose of a learning target is to provide clarity of learning for learners. Learning targets establish the goals of learning for the lesson.

Identify the standard(s) that you are addressing with the lesson and what students will learn.	
Identify how this learning target is connected to previous and future learning and why it is socially significant or important for students.	
Classify what students will learn from the lesson. (e.g. Blooms, Webb's Depth of Knowledge, Habits of Mind, etc.) *Examples: Students will know/reflect/understand/apply/use_____.*	
Plan for how students will know the learning target and what will they be doing to demonstrate understanding of the learning target. See <u>Success Criteria Guidelines</u>.	
Write the learning target in kid-friendly words, pictures, and/or actions.	
Communicate the learning target through verbal and/or visual strategies.	
Revisit the learning target throughout the lesson.	
Plan for how you will collect data on student mastery of the learning target for planning the next lesson (checks for understanding). See <u>Collecting Evidence of Student Progress</u>, <u>Formative Assessment Process</u>.	

References:

Moss, Connie M., & Brookhart, Susan M. (2012). *Learning targets: Helping students aim for understanding in today's lesson.* Alexandria, VA: ASCD.

5 Dimensions of Teaching and Learning, Instructional Framework 4.0, (2012). Center for Educational Leadership, University of Washington.

<u>Video: Communicating Learning Goals</u>

TABLE OF CONTENTS

ONE-PAGER

CHECKLIST

Success Criteria Guidelines

The purpose of success criteria is to describe the quality of work and discrete skills needed for students to meet the learning target in a way that students can understand and use for improvement.

Identify the standard(s) that you are addressing with the lesson and what students will learn.	
Identify how this learning target is connected to previous and future learning and why it is socially significant or important for students. How will students show evidence of learning and mastery of the learning target? See <u>Learning Targets</u>.	
Classify what students will learn from the lesson (e.g. Blooms, Webb's Depth of Knowledge, Habits of Mind, etc.). Think about whether the success criteria will be product or process oriented; developed by you or by students. 　　　*Examples: Students will know/reflect/understand/apply/use_____.*	
Develop (prior to the lesson or during the lesson with students) success criteria that capture how students will show evidence of learning.	
Plan for sharing the success criteria with learners. Will you demonstrate? Show a model? Name it only? Some possible phrasing: "I am successful if/when_____" or "The success criteria is _____".	
Check for student understanding of the success criteria.	
Plan for how you will collect data to ensure student mastery of the learning target. See <u>Formative Assessment</u>, <u>Formative Feedback</u>.	

References:
Moss, Connie M., & Brookhart, Susan M. (2012). *Learning targets: Helping students aim for understanding in today's lesson.* Alexandria, VA: ASCD.
5 Dimensions of Teaching and Learning, Instructional Framework 4.0, (2012). Center for Educational Leadership, University of Washington.

TABLE OF CONTENTS

ONE-PAGER

CHECKLIST

ASSESSMENT for STUDENT LEARNING

Formative Assessment Process Guidelines

The purpose of the formative assessment process is to use assessment-elicited evidence of students' progress for educators to adjust ongoing instructional procedures; for students to adjust their learning tactics and monitor their own progress over time.

Establish shared <u>learning target</u> and <u>success criteria</u>. [phase 1]	
Collect evidence of progress toward learning target that gives clear evidence of progress toward the learning target. This is an observable recording system of student progress. [phase 2]	
Communicate meaningful feedback that feeds learning forward and clearly tells students how well they are performing • effective feedback provides specific information that directly relates to the learning target and success criteria, the amount of progress made and where and how to proceed next. See <u>Formative Feedback Guidelines</u> & <u>Collecting Evidence of Student Progress</u>. [phase 3]	
Adjust instruction for whole group, small group and individuals based on evidence of progress toward the learning target. [phase 4]	
Provide opportunities for students to adjust learning strategies and tactics to meet learning target. [phase 4]	

References: Moss, Connie M., & Brookhart, Susan M. (2012). *Learning targets: Helping students aim for understanding in today's lesson.* Alexandria, VA: ASCD.

Moss, Connie M., & Brookhart, Susan M. (2009). *Advancing Formative Assessment in Every Classroom.* Alexandria, VA: ASCD.

Popham, James W. (2008). *Transformative assessment.* Alexandria, VA: ASCD.

5 Dimensions of Teaching and Learning, Instructional Framework 4.0, (2012). Center for Educational Leadership, University of Washington.

<u>Video about using clickers as a Formative Assessment tool</u>

Some Structures for collecting formative assessment data:
- write on/wipe off boards
- value line
- ticket out the door
- 3-2-1
- 6 word summary
- response cards
- freeze frame, tableau, vignettes
- running records
- checklists
- 4 corners
- <u>53 Ways to Check for Understanding</u>

<u>Video: Use Formative Assessment to Differentiate Instruction</u>
<u>VIdeo: Listening and Speaking: Formative Assessment</u>

CHECKLIST

Quality Questioning Guidelines

The purpose of questioning is to develop substantive intellectual thinking and talk; probe and deepen students' understanding; and uncover misconceptions that can be addressed with instruction, feedback, and practice.

Relate questions to the <u>learning target</u>.	
Vary style and complexity of questions *(i.e. Bloom's Level of Questions, Walsh and Sattes' Criteria for Quality Questions, Webb's Depth of Knowledge, open and closed questions, etc.)*	
Consider format in which students will respond to questions (orally, written, incorporated technology, whole group, small group, pairs, triads, etc.).	
Provide sufficient wait-time. Sufficient wait time is when every student has the opportunity to respond to the question.	
Offer explicit feedback through redirecting, probing, and responding when a student's response is incomplete or inaccurate. Use feedback to build a mistake friendly culture. See <u>Formative Feedback</u>.	
Use scaffolds to support students to bridge gap between current ability and the intended goal.	
Celebrate misconceptions as a learning opportunity. "I'm so glad you shared that thinking."	
Encourage students to ask their own questions and those of their peers.	

Resources:

Knight, Jim. (2013). *High impact instruction: A framework for great teaching.* Thousand Oaks, CA: 2013.

5 Dimensions of Teaching and Learning, Instructional Framework 4.0, (2012). Center for Educational Leadership, University of Washington.

5 Dimensions of Teaching and Learning, Instructional Framework 4.0, (2012). Center for Educational Leadership, University of Washington.

<u>Video: Using Open and Closed Questions</u>
<u>Video: Designing Questions</u>
<u>Video: Closed or Open: That is the Question</u>

TABLE OF CONTENTS

ONE-PAGER

CHECKLIST

Thinking Strategies Guidelines

The purpose of thinking strategies is for students to engage in habits of thinking that develop conceptual understanding and be able to transfer those habits of thinking to materials other than today's content.

Identify the thinking strategy appropriate for the day's lesson.
    1 - Critical Thinking - Analyze, Evaluate, Problem Solve
    2 - Creative Thinking - Generate, Associate, Hypothesize
    3 - Complex Thinking - Clarify, Interpret, Determine
    4 - Comprehensive Thinking - Understand, Infer, Compare
    5 - Collaborative Thinking - Explain, Develop, Decide
    6 - Communicative Thinking - Reason, Connect, Represent
    7 - Cognitive Transfer of Thinking - Synthesize, Generalize, Apply*
*this is not a definitive list of thinking strategies	

Highlight the steps associated with the thinking strategy.	
Give tips and coaching pointers to students as you model, explain, and demonstrate the strategy.	
Have students practice with feedback, and an opportunity to apply that feedback. See Formative Feedback.	
Evaluate how the students are doing with the thinking skill.	
Adjust instruction for whole group, small group and individuals based on evidence of mastery of the thinking strategy.	
Provide opportunities for students to adjust learning strategies and tactics to master the thinking strategy.	

Resources:

Harvey, S., & Goudvis A. (2007). *Strategies that work: Teaching comprehension for understanding and engagement.* 2nd ed. Portland, ME: Stenhouse.

Keene, Ellin O., & Zimmerman, S. (2007). *Mosaic of thought; the power of comprehension strategies.* Portsmouth, NH: Heinemann.

5 Dimensions of Teaching and Learning, Instructional Framework 4.0, (2012). Center for Educational Leadership, University of Washington.

Video: Elementary Engineering: From Simple Machines to Life Skills

TABLE OF CONTENTS

ONE-PAGER

CHECKLIST

CLASSROOM ENVIRONMENT & CULTURE

Culturally Responsive Teaching

The purpose of culturally responsive teaching is to create a culture of inclusivity, equity, and learning that ensures more of our students, including those historically underserved, engage and achieve at higher levels without having to give up who they are. This means that teaching points are relevant and meaningful; and based in students' life experiences, culture, and language. The foundation of culturally responsive teaching is positive relationships; teacher to student and student to student. Essential to culturally responsive teaching is seeing cultural differences as assets and challenging racial, religious, and cultural stereotypes and other forms of intolerance that are harmful.

Students are affirmed in their cultural connections. See <u>Affirming Cultural Identities</u>.	
Educators are personally inviting; they develop and maintain relationships that foster student well being and indicate that all are valued. See <u>Fostering Positive Relationships</u>.	
Learning environments are physically and culturally inviting. See <u>Culturally Responsive Learning Environment</u>.	
Students are reinforced for academic development. See <u>Emphasizing Academic Growth</u>.	
Educators use strategies that differentiate for individual strengths and needs. See <u>Differentiating Instruction</u>.	
Classrooms are managed with firm, consistent, caring control. See <u>Consistent, Attentive, Classroom Management</u>.	
Classroom interactions and learning opportunities are a balance of collective and individual structures. See <u>Discussion and Collaboration Routines</u>.	

Resources:
Gay, Geneva. (2010). *Culturally Responsive Teaching: Theory, research and practice.* New York: NY: Teachers College.
Howard, G. (2015). *We can't teach what we won't lead.* Thousand Oaks, CA: Corwin.
5 Dimensions of Teaching and Learning, Instructional Framework 4.0, (2012). Center for Educational Leadership, University of Washington.

TABLE OF CONTENTS

ONE-PAGER

CHECKLIST

MOMENTOUS INSTITUTE SCHOOL, DALLAS, TEXAS

Momentous is a small, urban, not-for-profit school just south of downtown Dallas, TX. Approximately 84% of their students qualify for free or reduced lunch, and 94% of their students are Latino, 4% are Black, and 2% are other races. Momentous focuses on social emotional health in their work with students as well as encouraging students to be "agents of change in their schools, communities, and the world."

Karen Norris, Director of Curriculum and Instruction, and Rhonda Vincent, Director of Educational Training, created their playbook by starting with that they call "The Essentials," the three components that work together in a Momentous classroom. They used their playbook to give life to each component.

They began the initial work in June of 2017, the playbook was introduced to staff in August of the same year, and they continue to work with teachers and coaches to revise and refine it.

The benefits of the playbook have been having clarity around best practices as well as making those practices explicitly tie to school culture. It has also led to "clarity in coaching conversations," according to Dr. Norris.

This excerpt of the Momentous Institute School Instructional Playbook is reprinted with permission of the Momentous Institute, Dallas, Texas. ©2018 Momentous Institute.

The Essentials Unpacked

- ❖ **Emotional Tone: Practices that make students feel safe, valued, confident, and optimistic**
  - ➢ **Relationship Building**
    - ■ Home Visit
    - ■ Morning Circle
    - ■ Closing Circle
  - ➢ **Lenses that Inform Practice**
    - ■ Trauma Informed
    - ■ Culturally Responsive
  - ➢ **Patterns of Interaction**
    - ■ Respectful
    - ■ Private, Proactive & Principled
  - ➢ **Explicit Instruction**
    - ■ Breathing Practice
    - ■ Teaching about the Brain
    - ■ Social Emotional Health Skills Lessons
- ❖ **Classroom Organization that make students feel honored, empowered and included.**
  - ➢ **Classroom Layout**
    - ■ Intentional Room Design
  - ➢ **Management**
    - ■ Expectations
    - ■ Routines and Procedures
  - ➢ **Responding to Student Behavior**
    - ■ Reinforcing Student Behavior
    - ■ The Discipline Conversation
    - ■ Choosing Appropriate Consequences
- ❖ **Instructional Practices that give students opportunities to take risks, explore, think deeply and develop a sense of themselves as learners.**
  - ➢ **Content Planning**
    - ■ UbD Units
    - ■ Project Based
    - ■ Learning Maps
    - ■ Essential Questions
  - ➢ **Continuous Assessment**
    - ■ Learning Targets
    - ■ Checks for Understanding
    - ■ Rubrics
    - ■ Ethic of Excellence
  - ➢ **Instruction**
    - ■ Thinking Routines
    - ■ Quality Questions
    - ■ Shared Learning
    - ■ Authentic Learning
    - ■ Field Trips

© Momentous Institute, (2017)   5

TABLE OF CONTENTS

ONE-PAGER

CHECKLIST

MORNING CIRCLE & CLOSING CIRCLE

IN ONE SENTENCE:
- Formatted activities used to provide social connection among class members at the beginning and end of each class day.

THE HATTIE CHECK:
- Teacher-student Relationships 0.72; Social Skills Program 0.40; Reducing Anxiety 0.40
- Participating in a Morning Circle and Closing Circle routine builds relationships in the classroom thus reducing student anxiety.
- Morning Circle and Closing Circle are designed to build Social Emotional Health Skills each day.

WHAT'S THE POINT:
- The beginning and ending of each day are important times of transition. These transitions can be both calm and meaningful when the morning and closing circle are established and practiced every day.

MORNING MEETING FORMAT
- Greeting
- Sharing
- Social Emotional Mini Lesson or Activity
- Breathing
- Daily Agenda

CLOSING CIRCLE FORMAT
- Breathing
- Closing Activity

HOW DOES MORNING MEETING & CLOSING CIRCLE BENEFIT THE TEACHER:
- Reduces the stress of transition time between home and school
- Begins and ends each day positively
- Teachers have a two daily opportunities to notice students' well-being
- Teachers have an established time to explicitly teach social emotional health skills
- Teachers have two daily opportunities to practice social emotional health skills and strategies with students.

HOW DOES MORNING MEETING & CLOSING CIRCLE BENEFIT THE STUDENT:
- These consistent and predictable practices make children feel secure.
- Students build and practice communication skills.
- Student have the opportunity to build and practice social emotional health skills daily.
- Building and practicing social emotional health skills during this consistent time lays the foundation for transferring these skills to other contexts.

© Momentous Institute, (2017)

9

TABLE OF CONTENTS

ONE-PAGER

CHECKLIST

MORNING CIRCLE & CLOSING CIRCLE

CHECKLIST: MORNING CIRCLE

CRITERIA	✓
The time for morning circle are a non-negotiable part of the classroom schedule.	
Morning circle activities are intentionally planned.	
Morning circle follows the prescribed format.	
Students exercise choice in selecting elements of the morning circle.	
Students exercise leadership of appropriate elements of the morning circle.	
Morning routines (turning in homework, putting away backpacks, lunch count, school-wide announcements, etc.) are conducted before the morning circle.	
The first academic task is started immediately after the morning circle.	

CHECKLIST: CLOSING CIRCLE

CRITERIA	✓
The time for closing circle are a non-negotiable part of the classroom schedule.	
Closing circle activities are intentionally planned.	
Closing circle follows the prescribed format.	
Students exercise choice in selecting elements of the closing circle.	
Students exercise leadership of appropriate elements of the closing circle.	
End of day routines (noting assignments, packing backpacks, end of day announcements, etc.) are conducted before the closing circle	
Classroom dismissal immediately follows the closing circle.	

TABLE OF CONTENTS

ONE-PAGER

CHECKLIST

TRAUMA INFORMED

IN ONE SENTENCE:
- Adopting a trauma informed lens allows teachers to understand how trauma and toxic stress can influence a child's ability to succeed in school.

THE HATTIE CHECK:
- Teacher Student Relationships 0.72; Classroom Management 0.52
- Being trauma informed helps teachers take perspective which impacts relationships and classroom management

WHAT'S THE POINT?
- The brains of traumatized children are often hyper vigilant, in a state of perpetual fight, flight or freeze, making learning difficult.

WHAT ARE THE CHARACTERISTICS OF A TRAUMA INFORMED TEACHER?
- The teacher
  - Is knowledgeable:
    - understands the long term impact of adverse childhood experience
    - understands how stress impacts brain function
    - understands neuroplasticity
  - Is safe
  - Is calm
  - Is consistent
  - Is patient
  - Is persistent
  - Is sensitive
  - Has empathy

HOW DOES TRAUMA OR TOXIC STRESS AFFECT THE STUDENTS?
- Often unable to:
  - Listen
  - Follow Directions or Rules
  - Concentrate or Focus
  - Learn at a typical pace
  - Be Patient
  - Develop and Maintain Productive and Enjoyable Relationships
  - Use Words to Get Needs Met
  - Take Turns
  - Exercise Self-Control
- Dysregulation from trauma or stress can lead to a negative self-image, deficient self-confidence, rigidity and an inability to deal with future challenges.

© Momentous Institute, (2017)   11

TABLE OF CONTENTS

ONE-PAGER

CHECKLIST

TRAUMA INFORMED

CHECKLIST: A TRAUMA INFORMED TEACHER

CRITERIA	✓
The Teacher	
Reviews the child's background to understand factors associated with trauma or toxic stress	
Documents behaviors to look for patterns	
Adapts his/her approach to fit the needs of the child	
Validates the students' perspectives	
Takes time to understand the source of problematic behavior	
Seeks assistance from available specialists	
Doesn't give up on the child	
uses strategies and tools to help students regulate	
Develops attainable goals to build child's capacity to self-regulate	
Celebrates success with the child	

TABLE OF CONTENTS

ONE-PAGER

CHECKLIST

CULTURALLY RESPONSIVE

IN ONE SENTENCE:
- Culturally responsive teaching provides all students with equitable opportunities for learning.

THE HATTIE CHECK:
- Teacher Student Relationships 0.72; Classroom Management 0.52

WHAT'S THE POINT?
- Acknowledging, responding to, and celebrating cultures provides equitable access to education for students from all cultures.

FIVE CHARACTERISTICS OF CULTURALLY RESPONSIVE TEACHING
- Positive perspectives on parents and families
- Communication of high expectation
- Learning within the context of culture
- Student centered instruction
- Culturally mediated Instruction

FOUR CONDITIONS NECESSARY FOR CULTURALLY RESPONSIVE TEACHING
- **Establish Inclusion**
  - Highlight the human purpose for what is being learned and its relationship to the students' lives
- **Develop Positive Attitude**
  - Relate teaching and learning to students' experience or previous knowledge
- **Enhance Meaning**
  - Provide challenging learning experiences and critical inquiry
- **Engender Competence**
  - Include multiple ways to represent knowledge and allow for self-assessment

REFERENCE:

Ladson-Billings, G. (1994). *The dreamkeepers*. San Francisco: Jossey-Bass Publishing Co.

Wlodkowski, R. J., and M. B. Ginsberg. (1995). *Diversity and Motivation: Culturally Responsive Teaching*. San Francisco: Jossey-Bass.

N.A. (2008). *Culturally responsive classroom management*. NY: New York University Steinhardt School of Culture, Education, and Human Development.

TABLE OF CONTENTS

ONE-PAGER

CHECKLIST

CULTURALLY RESPONSIVE

CHECKLIST: CULTURALLY RESPONSIVE TEACHER

CRITERIA	✓
The teacher:	
reflects upon own biases, attitudes and assumptions	
becomes knowledgeable of students' cultural backgrounds	
is sensitive to cultural differences in communication styles with students and parents	
is aware of and resists adopting stereotypes	
offers explicit expectations	
engages students in discussions about class norms	
models the expected behavior	
is aware of inconsistency in application of consequences	

CHECKLIST: CULTURALLY RESPONSIVE CLASSROOM

CRITERIA	✓
Display maps that highlight students' countries of origin	
Post signs or banners welcoming students in the language(s) they speak	
Display posters depicting people of various cultural groups	
Include books that promote themes of diversity, tolerance and community	
Design activities that allow students to work together and help each other	

14

TABLE OF CONTENTS

ONE-PAGER

CHECKLIST

INTENTIONAL ROOM DESIGN

IN ONE SENTENCE:
- Classroom spaces are designed to suit their purpose.

THE HATTIE CHECK:
- Reducing Anxiety 0.40
- Defining spaces for specific purpose let students know what kinds of task and activities will be accomplished in that space.

WHAT'S THE POINT:
- Intentionally designed classroom spaces maximizes efficiency of available space, establishes purposes for each area, and supports student learning.
- Intentional room design contributes to a student's sense of security and autonomy as they navigate spaces within the classroom.

HOW DO TEACHERS DESIGN CLASSROOMS:
- Teachers should spend time before the start of the school year thinking about the types of learning and community building that should occur in the classroom.
- In determining room design, teachers pay particular attention to how students should move, use their voices, take care of materials and interact with each other.
- Room design should facilitate both teaching and learning.

HOW DOES ROOM DESIGN BENEFIT STUDENTS:
- Students should feel as if the classroom was designed for them and to facilitate support their learning.
- Students will gain security as they recognize that there is a specific place for supplies, materials, and belongings.

TABLE OF CONTENTS

ONE-PAGER

CHECKLIST

INTENTIONAL ROOM DESIGN

CHECKLIST: QUALITY ROOM DESIGN - BEFORE THE FIRST DAY OF SCHOOL

CRITERIA	✓
Personal space for each student	
Large space for whole class gatherings	
Small group spaces	
Individual work spaces	
Teacher-guided small group space	
Calm-Down Space	
Place to turn in assignments	
Space between learning areas for ease of movement	
Community Wall or Bulletin Board	
Storage for Seldom-used materials	
Materials for student use are organized	
Materials for student use are accessible to students	
Procedures for proper organization and storage of materials	
Lighting sources include natural light and dim light	

CHECKLIST: QUALITY ROOM DESIGN - DURING THE SCHOOL YEAR

CRITERIA	✓
Photos of students learning and playing are posted	
Student work displayed on the community wall	
High quality student work displayed in the hallways	
Brief, student-written or teacher-scribed narratives accompany displayed work.	

© Momentous Institute, (2017)   27

TABLE OF CONTENTS

ONE-PAGER

CHECKLIST

UNDERSTANDING BY DESIGN (UbD)

IN ONE SENTENCE:
- The UbD framework provides a structure and a planning process for designing curriculum, assessment and Instruction.

THE HATTIE CHECK:
- Teacher Clarity 0.75; Goals 0.56
- Designing UbD units and unpacking learning standards (i.e. TEKS) ensures that teachers have clarity around learning goals.
- With clarity, teachers are able to design learning experiences to meet the identified goals.

WHAT'S THE POINT:
- The UbD framework focuses the curriculum and teaching on developing and deepening students' understanding and transfer of learning.
- Curriculum is planned backwards through a three-stage design process.
- This backward design ensures that textbooks are treated as resources and not the curriculum, and that the learning activities are intentionally chosen and have a clear purpose.

HOW DO TEACHERS USE THE UbD FRAMEWORK:
- Guided by standards, teachers craft the curriculum and learning experiences to meet specific purposes.
- Teachers design the formative assessments that reveal students' learning needs and guides teaching.
- Teachers design the summative assessment that reveals what the student understand, know and are able to do.
- In designing the curriculum, assessments and learning experiences, teachers are able to identify with clarity what a student should understand, know, and be able to do, and plan learning experiences that accomplish these goals.

HOW DO STUDENTS EXPERIENCE UbD:
- Students should feel the connected nature of a unit.
- All learning provides part of the answer to the Essential Questions.
- All learning helps them to be successful on the Performance Task.
- Much of the UbD framework is invisible to the students; however, students respond to the Essential Questions during the course of the unit and are exposed to the knowledge and skills through the Learning Targets.

REFERENCE:
Wiggins, G. & McTighe, J. (2005). *Understanding by design.* Alexandra, VA: Association for Supervision and Curriculum Development.

© Momentous Institute, (2017)   40

UbD UNIT

CHECKLIST: QUALITY UbD UNIT

CRITERIA	✓
Identifies the learning goals through the Understandings, Knowledge and Skill	
Includes formative and summative assessments, including Performance Tasks, aligned to the learning goals	
Identifies the key components of the learning plan	
Guides daily lesson planning	

CHECKLIST: USING UbD UNITS TO GUIDE LESSON PLANNING AND DAILY INSTRUCTION

CRITERIA	✓
Daily learning targets are pulled from the knowledge and skills identified in the unit	
Formative and Summative assessments address the daily learning targets	

CHECKLIST: UNIT MAINTENANCE - After Teaching a Unit

CRITERIA	✓
Knowledge & Skills are updated	
Assessments, including Performance Tasks are updated	
Learning activities are updated	
Resources are updated	
Lesson Plans are linked to the unit	

TABLE OF CONTENTS

ONE-PAGER

CHECKLIST

RUBRICS

IN ONE SENTENCE:
- A guide that lists cohesive criteria and includes descriptions of levels of performance quality on the criteria
-

THE HATTIE CHECK:
- Self Reported Grades 1.44; Teacher Clarity 0.75; Providing Formative Evaluation 0.90; Feedback 0.75
- Students know the criteria by which to evaluate their performance
- Rubrics help teacher avoid confusing completion of the task with learning
- Rubrics give students clarity on what they still need to learn
- Rubrics provide specific feedback

WHAT'S THE POINT:
- Rubric give students clarity on the qualities their work should have.
- Rubrics help teachers focus on the criteria not the task
- Rubric fit solidly within the knowledge, doing, reflecting cycle which is part of a comprehensive assessment system

CREATING AND USING RUBRICS:
- When creating rubrics teachers should focus on the criteria by which learning will be assessed.
- As teachers create rubrics, learning outcomes and content is clarified.
- Rubrics are used to assess student performance.
- Teachers should present the rubric to the students at the beginning of instruction so that students have opportunities to compare their work to the criteria

HOW DOES USING RUBRICS BENEFIT THE STUDENTS?
- Rubric help students understand what the desired performance is and what it looks like.
- Students are able to determine the quality of the performance when compared to the criteria listed on the rubric.
- Students are able to use feedback from the rubrics to revise or move on to another task before receiving a final grade.

REFERENCE:
Brookhart, S. M. (2013). *How to create and use rubrics for formative assessment and grading.* Alexandra, VA: Association for Supervision and Curriculum Development.

52

TABLE OF CONTENTS   ONE-PAGER   CHECKLIST

RUBRICS

DESIGNING QUALITY RUBRICS

CRITERIA	✓
Focuses on the criteria that will be assessed; what student will learn not what you will teach	
Aligned with the learning goals and targets of the unit	
Clarifies for students the qualities their work should have	
Includes description of the criteria	
Includes the quality levels that will demonstrate learning	

USING RUBRICS WITH STUDENTS

CRITERIA	✓
Introduce the rubric when the performance is introduced.	
Students use the rubric to define the qualities their work should have.	
Students compare their work with the quality levels detailed on the rubric.	
Students revise based on the feedback they get when they apply the rubric to their work.	
Students use the rubrics to self-evaluate.	

TABLE OF CONTENTS

ONE-PAGER

CHECKLIST

QUALITY QUESTIONS

IN ONE SENTENCE:
- Questions designed to engage students in interactions with teachers and peers around the content and to increase their understanding and mastery of curriculum.

THE HATTIE CHECK:
- Classroom discussion 0.82; Teacher-student relationships 0.72; Questioning 0.48
- Quality Questions engage students in stimulating classroom discussion
- Teachers spend 30-50% of their time asking question (Cotton, 1989). Shouldn't these questions deepen student understanding?

WHAT'S THE POINT:
- Quality Questions promote thinking, initiate reflection, scaffolds student understanding, identifies gaps, fosters deeper thinking, and increases engagement.

TYPES OF QUESTIONS:
- **Hook Question**
  - Is intentionally designed to spark student curiosity or interest
  - Lies at the heart of the lesson or unit
- **Diagnostic Question**
  - Addresses a critical component of unit and lesson design
  - Formed around concepts and skills with which previous classes had difficulty
- **Questions to Check Understanding**
  - Used as formative assessment or when teacher senses that students are not following the lesson and decides to verify this in order to adjust instruction.
- **Probing Question**
  - Usually emerges during a teacher to student interaction
  - Focuses on the part of the student response that was incorrect, incomplete or unclear
- **Inference Questions**
  - Requires students to use evidence to draw conclusions
  - Asks students to synthesize information
- **Transfer Question**
  - Requires student to apply knowledge in a novel setting
- **Predictive Question**
  - Engages student in if-then thinking, is open-ended, and there is no one right answer
- **Reflective Question**
  - Asks students assess their own understanding of the content they are learning and encourages student ownership of their learning

REFERENCE:
Walsh, J. A. & Sattes, B. D. (2011). *Thinking through quality questioning: Deepening student engagement.* Thousand Oaks, CA: Corwin.
Knight. J. (2013). *High impact instruction.* Thousand Oaks, CA: Corwin.

© Momentous Institute, (2017)   56

TABLE OF CONTENTS

ONE-PAGER

CHECKLIST

QUALITY QUESTIONS

CHECKLIST: QUALITY QUESTIONS

CRITERIA	✓
Promote one or more carefully defined instructional purpose	
Focus on important content	
Facilitate thinking at various cognitive level	
Communicate clearly what is being asked	
Crafted during lesson planning	

CHECKLIST: USING QUALITY QUESTIONS WITH STUDENTS

CRITERIA	✓
Ask questions of all students	
Practice wait time 1 & 2	
Use repeat, rephrase, reduce, reach out	
Avoid giving away the answers	
Hold student accountable	

© Momentous Institute, (2017)   57

TABLE OF CONTENTS

ONE-PAGER

CHECKLIST

REFERENCES

Ainsworth, L., & Viegut, D. (2014). *Common formative assessments 2.0: How teacher teams intentionally align standards, instruction, and assessment*. Thousand Oaks, CA: Corwin Press.

Almarode, J., Fisher, D., Frey, N., & Hattie, J. (2018). *Visible learning for science: What works best to optimize student learning*. Thousand Oaks, CA: Corwin Press.

Amabile, T., & Kramer, S. (2011). *The progress principle: Using small wins to ignite joy, engagement, and creativity at work*. Boston, MA: Harvard Business Review Press.

Agryris, C. (2005, March). Actionable Knowledge. In C. Knudsen & Tsoukas. H. (Eds.), *The Oxford handbook of organization theory* (pp. 423-452.) Oxford, UK: Oxford University

Atwell, N. (2014). *In the middle: New understandings about writing, reading, and learning*. London, UK: Heinemann.

Beers, K. (2003). *When kids can't read: What teachers can do*. London, UK: Heinemann.

Black, P., & Wiliam, D. (1998). Inside the black box: Raising standards through classroom assessment. *Phi Delta Kappan*, 80, 139-148.

Boaler, J. (2015). *Mathematical mindsets: Unleashing students' potential through creative math, inspiring messages and innovative teaching.* San Francisco, CA: Jossey-Bass.

Boaler, J., Munson, J., & Williams, C. (2019). *Mindset mathematics: Visualizing and investigating big ideas, grade 6.* San Francisco, CA: Jossey-Bass.

Brown, B. (2006, January). Shame resilience theory: A grounded theory study on women and shame. *Families in Society: The Journal of Contemporary Human Services*, 87(1), 43-52.

Bulgren, J., Deshler, D., & Lenz, B. K. (2007, March). Engaging adolescents with LD in higher order thinking about history concepts using integrated content enhancement routines. *US National Library of Medicine National Institutes of Health*, 40(2), 121-133.

Bulgren, J. A., Lenz, B. K., Schumaker, J. B., Deshler, D. D., & Marquis, J. G. (2002). The use and effectiveness of a comparison routine in diverse secondary content classrooms. *Journal of Educational Psychology*, 94, 356-371.

Burgess, D. (2012). *Teach like a pirate: Increase student engagement, boost your creativity, and transform your life as an educator.* San Diego, CA: Dave Burgess Consulting, Incorporated.

Center for Applied Linguistics. (n.d.). *The SIOP model.* Washington, DC: Author.

Camerer, C., Loewenstein, G., & Weber, M. (1989). The curse of knowledge in economic settings: An experimental analysis. *Journal of Political Economy*, 97(5), 1232-1254.

Chappuis, J. (2014). *Seven strategies of assessment for learning – edition 2*. New York, NY: Pearson.

Clance, P. R., & Imes, S. A. (1978). The impostor phenomenon in high achieving women: Dynamics and therapeutic intervention. *Psychotherapy Theory, Research and Practice*, 15(3), 241-247.

Coe, R. (2002, September). It's the effect size, stupid: What effect size is and why it is important. Paper presented at the British Educational Research Association annual conference, Exeter, UK.

Columbo, B., Deshler, D. D., Schumacher, J. B., & Tralli, R. (1996). The strategies intervention model: A model for supported inclusion at the secondary level. *Remedial and Special Education*, 17(4), 204-216.

Covey, S. (1989). *The 7 habits of highly effective people*. Miami, FL: FranklinCovey.

Daniels, H., & Harvey, S. (2015). *Comprehension and collaboration: Inquiry circles for curiosity, engagement and understanding*. London, UK: Heinemann.

Davenport, T. H. (2005). *Thinking for a living: How to get better performance and results from knowledge workers*. Boston, MA: Harvard Business School Press.

Davis, J. H., & Lawrence-Lightfoot, S. (1997). *The art and science of portraiture*. San Francisco, CA: Jossey-Bass Publishers.

Dean, C. B., Hubbell, E. R., Pitler, H., & Stone, B. (2012). *Classroom instruction that works: Research-based strategies for increasing student achievement (2nd ed.)*. Alexandria, VA: Association for Supervision and Curriculum Development.

Deci, E. L., Koestner, R., & Ryan, R. M. (1999, November). A meta-analytic review of experiments examining the effects of extrinsic rewards on intrinsic motivation. *Psychological Bulletin*, 125(6), 627-668.

Deci, E. L., & Ryan, R. M. (2000). *Intrinsic motivation and self-determination in human behavior.* New York, NY: Plenum.

Deshler, D. D., & Schumaker, J. B. (1988). An instructional model for teaching students how to learn. In J. L. Graden, J. E. Zins, & M. J. Curtis (Eds.), *Alternative educational delivery systems: Enhancing instructional options for all students* (pp. 391-411). Washington, DC: National Association of School Psychologists.

Drucker, P. F. (1969). *The age of discontinuity: Guidelines to our changing society.* London, UK: Heinemann.

Edmondson, A. C. (2019). *The fearless organization: Creating psychological safety in the workplace for learning, innovation, and growth.* Hoboken, NJ: John Wiley & Sons, Inc.

Fisher, D. B., Frey, N., & Hattie, J. (2016). *Teaching literacy in the visible learning classroom, grades K-5, edition 1.* Thousand Oaks, CA: Corwin.

Fisher, D. B., Frey, N., Quaglia, R. J., Smith, D., & Lande, L. (2017). *Engagement by design: Creating learning environments where students thrive.* Thousand Oaks, CA: Corwin Press.

Friere, P. (1970). *Pedagogy of the oppressed.* New York, NY: Bloomsbury.

Fullan, M. (2001). *Principals as leaders in a culture of change.* Toronto, ONT: University of Toronto, Ontario Institute for Studies in Education.

Gaiman, N. (2017). The Neil story. Retrieved from http://journal. neilgaiman.com/2017/05/the-neil-story-with-additional-footnote.html

Gallagher, K. (2004). *Deeper reading: Comprehending challenging texts, 4-12.* Portsmouth, NH: Stenhouse Publishers.

Gallagher, K. (2011). *Write like this: Teaching real-world writing through modeling and mentor texts.* Portsmouth, NH: Stenhouse Publishers.

Garrison, M., Howard, H. M., & Sprick, R. (2009). *CHAMPS: A proactive and positive approach to classroom management.* Eugene, OR: Pacific Northwest Publishing.

Gawande, A. (2007). *Better: A surgeon's notes on performance.* New York, NY: Metropolitan Books.

Gawande, A. (2009). *The Checklist Manifesto: How to get things right.* New York, NY: Metropolitan Books.

Gladwell, M. (2002). *Tipping point: How little ideas can make a big difference.* New York, NY: Little, Brown and Company.

Glaser, J. E. (2016). *Conversational intelligence: How great leaders build trust and get extraordinary results.* New York, NY: Bibliomotion, Inc.

Godin, S. (2012). *The Icarus deception: How high will you fly?* New York, NY: Penguin Group.

Goleman, D. (2013, December). The focused leader. *Harvard Business Review.*

Goudvis, A., & Harvey, S. (2017). *Strategies that work: Teaching comprehension for engagement, understanding, and building knowledge, grades K-8.* Portsmouth, NH: Stenhouse Publishers.

Grant Halvorson, H. (2012). *Nine things successful people do differently.* Boston, MA: Harvard Business Review Press.

Hammond, Z. L. (2015). *Culturally responsive teaching and the brain: Promoting authentic engagement and rigor among culturally and linguistically diverse students.* Thousand Oaks, CA: Corwin Publishers.

Hattie, J. (2008). *Visible learning: A synthesis of over 800 meta-analyses relating to achievement.* New York, NY: Routledge.

Hattie, J. (2012). *Visible learning for teachers: Maximizing impact on learning.* New York, NY: Routledge.

Hattie, J., Fisher, D., Frey, N., Gojak, L. M., Moore, S. D., & Mellman, W. (2016). *Visible learning for mathematics, grades K-12: What works best to optimize student learning.* Thousand Oaks, CA: Corwin Press.

Hattie, J., & Zierer, K. (2017). *10 mindframes for visible learning: Teaching for success.* New York, NY: Routledge.

Heath, C., & Heath, D. (2010). *Switch: How to change things when change is hard.* New York, NY: Random House.

Hollister, R., & Watkins, M. D. (2018, September-October). Too many projects. *Harvard Business Review,* 64-71.

Homer, T., Huang, T., Lee, Y., Schroder, C. M., & Scott, T. P. (2007). A meta-analysis of national research: Effects of teaching strategies on student achievement in science in the United States. *Journal of Research in Science Teaching, 44*(10), 1436-1460.

James, W. (1890). *The principles of psychology.* New York, NY: H. Holt and Company.

Jensen, B. (2001). *Simplicity: The new competitive advantage in a world of more, better, faster.* New York, NY: Perseus Books.

Johnson, A. W., & Johnson, R. (2013). Cooperative learning methods: A meta-analysis. *Journal of Research in Education, 12*(1), 5-14.

Johnson, S. (2018). *Farsighted: How we make the decisions that matter the most.* New York, NY: Penguin Random House.

Kagan, M., & Kagan, S. (2009). *Kagan cooperative learning.* San Clemente, CA: Kagan.

Keene. E. O. (2018). *Engaging children: Igniting a drive for deeper learning.* London, UK: Heinemann.

Knight, J. (2007). *Instructional coaching: A partnership approach to improving instruction.* Thousand Oaks, CA: Corwin.

Knight, J., Cornett, J., Skrtic, T., Kennedy, M., Novosel, L., & Mitchell, B. (2010, April). *Understanding attributes of effective coaches.* Paper presented at the annual meeting of the American Educational Research Association, San Diego, CA.

Knight, J. (2011). *Unmistakable impact: A partnership approach for dramatically improving instruction.* Thousand Oaks, CA: Corwin.

Knight, J. (2013). *High-impact instruction: A framework for great teaching.* Thousand Oaks, CA: Corwin.

Knight, J. (2014). *Focus on teaching: Using video for high-impact instruction.* Thousand Oaks, CA: Corwin.

Knight, J. (2017). *The Impact Cycle: What Instructional Coaches Should Do to Foster Powerful Improvements in Teaching.* Thousand Oaks, CA: Corwin.

Knight, J. (2019). Instructional coaching for implementing Visible Learning: A model for translating research into practice. *Education Sciences,* 9 (101).

Kondo, M., & Hirano, C. (2014). *The life-changing magic of Tidying up: The Japanese art of decluttering and organizing (first American edition.).* Berkeley, CA: Ten Speed Press.

Korda, A., Reed, C., & Selznick, D. O. (Producers) & Reed, C. (Director). (1949). *The third man* [Motion picture]. London, UK: London Films.

Laing, R. D. (1972). *Knots.* London, UK: Tavistock Publications Limited.

Lauer, P. A. (2006). *An education research primer: How to understand, evaluate, and use it.* San Francisco, CA: Jossey-Bass.

Learning Sciences Marzano Center. (2017). *Learning map, scales and evidences for the Marzano focused teacher evaluation model.* West Palm Beach, FL: Learning Sciences International.

Lefever, L. (2013). *The Art of Explanation: Making Your Ideas, Products, and Services Easier to Understand.* Hoboken, NJ: John Wiley & Sons, Inc.

LeMov, D. (2010). *Teach like a champion: 49 techniques that put students on the path to college.* San Francisco, CA: Jossey-Bass Teacher.

LeMov, D. (2015). *Teach like a champion: 62 Techniques that put students on the path to college.* San Francisco, CA: Jossey-Bass.

Lencioni, P. (2002). *The five dysfunctions of a team: A leadership fable.* San Francisco, CA: Jossey-Bass.

Lincoln, Y. S., & Guba, E. G. (1985). *Naturalistic inquiry* London, UK: Sage Publications.

Lopez, S. (2014). *Making hope happen: Create the future you want for yourself and others.* New York, NY: Atria.

Lui, E. (2006). *Guiding lights: How to mentor – and find life's purpose.* New York: NY: Ballantine Books.

Marzano, R., Pickering, D. J., & Pollock, J. E. (2001). *Classroom instruction that works: Research-based strategies for increasing student achievement.* Alexandria, VA: Association for Supervision and Curriculum Development.

Marzano, R. J. (2017). *The new art and science of teaching: More than 50 new instructional strategies for student success.* Iowa City, IA: Solution Tree Press.

National Council of Teachers of Mathematics. (2014). *Principles to actions: Ensuring mathematical success for all.* Washington, DC: Author.

Nonaka, I., & Takeuchi, H. (1995). *The knowledge creating company.* Boston, MA: Harvard Business Review.

Parker, J. P. (2009, March-April). The broken-open heart: Living with faith and hope in the tragic gap. *A Journal of the Christian Spiritual Life, pp. 1-12.*

Parrish, S. (2010). *Number talks: Helping children build mental math and computation strategies, grades K-5.* Sausalito, CA: Math Solutions.

Polanyi, M. (1966). *The tacit dimension.* Chicago, IL: University of Chicago Press.

Pressfield, S. (2002). *The war of art: Winning the inner creative battle.* New York, NY: Black Irish Entertainment.

Prochaska, J. O., Norcross, J. C., & DiClemente, C. C., & (1994). *Changing for good: A revolutionary six-stage program for overcoming bad habits and moving your life positively forward.* New York, NY: Harper Collins Publishers.

Reinhardt, A. (1998, May 25). Apple. *BusinessWeek.*

Sandberg, S. (2013). *Lean in: Women, work, and the will to lead.* New York, NY: Alfred A. Knopf.

Saphier, J., Haley-Speca, & Gower R. (2007). *Skillful teacher: Building your teaching skills (6th ed.).* Acton, MA: Research for Better Teaching.

Schlechty, P. C. (2011). *Engaging students: The next level of working on the work.* San Francisco, CA: Jossey-Bass.

Sencibaugh, J. M. (2007). Meta-analysis of reading comprehension interventions for students with learning disabilities: Strategies and implications. *Reading Improvement, 44(1), 6-22.*

Smith, M. S., & Stein, M. K. (2018). *Five practices for orchestrating productive mathematics discussions*. Thousand Oaks, CA: Corwin.

Smith, M., & Sherin, M. G. (2019). *The five practices in practice: Successfully orchestrating mathematics discussions in your middle school classroom*. Thousand Oaks, CA: Corwin.

Sousa, D. A. (2014). *How the brain learns mathematics*. Thousand Oaks, CA: Corwin Press.

Sprick, R. (2009). *CHAMPS: A proactive and positive approach to classroom management*. Eugene, OR: Pacific Northwest Publishing, Inc.

Stanier, M. B. (2016). *The coaching habit: Say less, ask more & change the way you lead forever*. Toronto, ONT: Box of Crayons Press.

Stiggins, R. (2000). *Student-involved classroom assessment*. New York, NY: Prentice Hall.

Tapper, J. (2012). *Solving for why: Understanding, assessing, and teaching students who struggle with math, grades K-8*. Sausalito, CA: Math Solutions Publications.

Tomlinson, C. A. (2014). *The differentiated classroom: Responding to the needs of all learners*. Alexandria, VA: Association for Supervision and Curriculum Development.

Wiggins, G. & McTighe, J. (2005). *Understanding by design*. Alexandria, VA: Association for Supervision and Curriculum Development.

Wiliam, D., & Leahy, S. (2015). *Embedding formative assessment: Practical techniques for K-12 classrooms*. West Palm Beach, FL: Learning Sciences International.